IT'S NEVER JUST BUSINESS

IT'S NEVER JUST BUSINESS

IT'S ABOUT *PEOPLE*

J. SCOTT

LIONCREST
PUBLISHING

IT'S NEVER JUST BUSINESS
It's about People

ISBN   978-1-5445-0224-3 *Paperback*
       978-1-5445-0225-0 *Ebook*

To my wife, Colleen, who had no idea what she was getting into when she married an entrepreneur. She has been there to pick me up when I was down and to celebrate every win. She has been my companion on a journey without any way to influence the outcome. Thank you for sticking with me and for giving me the two loves of my life!

CONTENTS

INTRODUCTION 9

PART ONE: LEADERSHIP: IT ISN'T ABOUT YOU
1. LEADERSHIP VERSUS AUTHORITY....................27
2. WHEN LEADERSHIP IS NECESSARY....................59
3. LEADERSHIP REQUIRES PREPARATION............83
4. LEADERS NEED LEADERSHIP 105
5. MEETINGS ARE WHERE WE LEAD 123

PART TWO: COMMUNICATION IS A VEHICLE, NOT A SCAPEGOAT
6. WE COMMUNICATE TO LEAD............................157
7. TAKE RESPONSIBILITY FOR WHAT'S HEARD...................179

PART THREE: A CULTURE OF ACCOUNTABILITY
8. ACCOUNTABILITY IS GENEROUS AND KIND.....................199

CONCLUSION...217
ACKNOWLEDGMENTS.......................................221
ABOUT THE AUTHOR.......................................223

INTRODUCTION

Most people that find themselves in a leadership role want to do something awesome and be impactful in the world. The funny thing about leadership is that it's hard; real leadership goes against most of the instincts that kept us alive before the modern age. The hard truth is that leadership isn't about you. Great leaders put their personal agenda aside to ensure their team members succeed first. If you are playing for your own success, you are a **BOSS**, not a leader.

The other thing about leadership is that being a boss is way easier than being a leader. Bozos get promoted every day; hard-hitting assholes are celebrated by Wall Street and Hollywood. So why do you want to be a leader? Because leaders change things; they push the human race forward. Leaders inspire those around them to reach for greatness. And leaders prove that extraordinary leadership does not require official authority, it simply requires that we put the prosperity of our stakeholders first.

Leadership is messy and involves making mistakes, which can turn into the greatest growth opportunities. Rarely will you learn something from a good decision, because you got lucky with your first guess. You learn when you get it wrong and have to acknowledge, analyze the situation, and guess again. And the cycle repeats. Learning from mistakes involves allowing your preexisting beliefs to be challenged. "This is how we have always done it" works when it's working, but not when you aren't getting the results you want. The first step to becoming a great leader is to celebrate your mistakes and those of your team members and learn everything you can from them.

While leadership is hard and you will learn the most from your and your team's mistakes, this book is intended to make that gap smaller for you. If you're trying to build a company, build an organization, keep up with the innovation required to be competitive today, or just trying to change the world, you're going to make mistakes. My goal is to share mine with you, so you don't have to fail as many times as I did to become the effective leader you aspire to be. In the pages that follow, I will share my train wrecks, my lessons learned, and my triumphs. Please make sure your seat belt is securely fastened and your tray table is in the upright position.

MY EARLY VIEW OF LEADERSHIP

I grew up in a pretty tough neighborhood as an outcast. I was one of five white kids in a gangland neighborhood of Los Angeles and was only five years old when I saw my first murder. My parents separated, and my dad moved to Colorado. I hated school from the fifth grade on and finally dropped out of high school in the eleventh grade to join the Navy and see the world.

I was in the Navy six years, two months, and twenty-three days, and I was wildly successful. I spent nine months in the Persian Gulf during Desert Shield/Desert Storm and received a Navy Achievement Medal for Leadership. After the war, I volunteered for anything and everything. My motto was "say YES!" One of the highlights was when I became a rescue swimmer, because the search and rescue school has the second highest attrition rate of all the special forces. My only motivation to go to SAR school was to see if I could get through it. When I graduated, I remember thinking, *I can't believe I did it!*

As I transitioned into corporate America, my view of leadership was founded on the power paradigm of gangland leaders, naval officers, and what I had seen watching actors on television and in movies. *Top Gun*. *Rambo*. *Wall Street*. I thought these were leaders. They gave orders and people followed them. It wasn't until much later that I realized these people weren't leaders at all. They were **bosses**, and they succeeded at the expense of other people or by dictating their actions.

When I transitioned out of the military, I went to work at Universal Studios in tech support. Within a year I was promoted to director and was tasked with managing national technology rollouts. I was there four years and wrapped up my tenure by rescuing their global Y2K project. I took over the project in March of 1999, with only nine months left before the New Year, and the team in place was still only in planning mode. My team had to touch every piece of technology in over 127 offices worldwide, including the theme parks. This included computers, data centers, and even the equipment that controlled the roller coasters.

We completed the worldwide remediation efforts in November of 1999. The project was a success, and I wanted more! I had been working with project managers from some of the largest global consulting firms, and I found that I had to teach them how to do their jobs. They were billing Universal $200 per hour for their services and I was on salary at $80,000. It was clear there was demand for a project management firm that could deliver results, so I started one. My goal was simple: I was going to be the best in the business and make tons of money.

GROWING A COMPANY...THE WRONG WAY

When I first started my project management firm, 120VC, I was the only employee. For the first couple of years, that was exactly what I wanted. As time went on, my clients started asking me to take on more and more, to the point where I had to start saying no. I was already working sixty- to eighty-hour weeks and didn't think I could continue to be successful if I increased my workload.

As most of you know, saying no is a bummer. According to William Ury, "no" is one of the hardest things for most people to say. Instead of continuing to say no, I decided I was going to start a real company and start hiring employees. So I started telling my customers I could bring in other consultants that would deliver "just like me." They were skeptical at first but needed the work done, so after five years of working independently, I took on my first staff member.

I didn't know it at the time, but I had lied when I said they would deliver "just like me."

As I started to expand, I required my staff to come to me for every decision because I believed I was the best at what we did, and it was my name on the door. To an extent, I *was* the best at what we did, and customer fulfillment was important to me. I had promised my clients that as I hired other people to take on their projects, my staff would continue to exceed their expectations just like I did.

That was naïve, and I essentially lied to them. They didn't know it, and the lie wasn't intentional; in reality, though, it's impossible to duplicate yourself. Believe me, I tried. As I hired people it was my way or the highway. I trained them to come to me for every little thing until my time was now at capacity again. I woke up one morning with five conflicting thoughts: I had achieved my goal, I was one of the best in the business, I made a ton of money, my job was a total grind, and I was the architect of my own situation.

I called an all-hands meeting and shared how I was feeling with my team. I encouraged them to tell me what sucked about 120VC—the best and worst decision I had made to that point. It was the best decision because they told me; they gave me the opportunity to hear them and make the company a better place to work. It was the worst decision because I was entirely emotionally unprepared to listen to my staff tell me how ugly my baby was.

I had reached a point in the development of the business where I knew even though I was smart, capable, and good at what I did, I was the only one coming up with new ideas. Therefore, the company was only as smart as me. My leadership style required a shift. I had to figure out how to live up to my client commitments, scale the business, work with my staff, help them make decisions, and still have the company go in the direction I wanted it to go. The task seemed daunting. How could I let everybody make decisions and still stay in control? The answer was simple: I couldn't. I was still a boss; I wasn't yet a leader.

Leaders help their team self-actuate a roadmap to a shared goal. They believe everyone is equal and enlightened. You can't fake this. You have to truly believe that even if someone doesn't have the same IQ or isn't as accomplished as you are, they are truly your equal. You don't have to be a genius to be an innovator, and you don't have to be a thought leader to be capable of great things.

As you can imagine, my company and I didn't transform overnight. When I asked my team to start making decisions autonomously, they didn't trust me immediately. In fact, they responded to my demand to "bring solutions instead of problems" by bringing multiple solutions without any opinion on which would be the best to solve the problem they faced. They wanted me to decide. I realized later that the bigger problem was that

I had hired people that didn't want to take responsibility. They wanted a boss and I had hired these people because I *was* a boss.

My biggest lesson from that time was that leaders don't really create a culture, we hire it. I was a boss, so I screened for smart, capable people that I thought would do what I said. When I decided to be a leader instead of a boss, I struggled to get most of my staff to step up.

Weird, right?

Nope!

So I started hiring people that I thought would take responsibility, work autonomously, and generate ideas to help grow the company. They didn't stay long at first, and I didn't understand why.

TIME FOR CHANGE

When the company stalled, we were at $10 million in annual revenue, seventy employees, and had fifteen Fortune 100 clients in the Los Angeles/Orange County area. For the first time, I had unhappy clients and I couldn't put out all of the fires. I was a high school dropout who had started a company, and I needed a real CEO.

My aha moment...I had been winging it the whole time. I was betting the company on my belief that I was talented and would always have the right answer, instead of seeking knowledge and studying the success and failures of the leaders that came before me. And my staff was incapable of original thinking or bringing in new clients without my help. I finally realized that if I wasn't growing, neither was my company. In other words, if the company was stalled, it's because I had stalled. I needed to become a voracious learner!

I began doing research and reading everything I could get my hands on. I joined Vistage, a CEO community that gave me a coach and a CEO peer group. I started getting serious about learning how to be a CEO. I learned that a leader doesn't make decisions for others—the distinction between an authority and a leader. I was the founder and CEO and held all the authority. I could tell people to do something and they would, hopefully out of respect and admiration, but that's not what a leader does.

Today, after a lot of trial and error, I consider myself a leader and offer my team members purpose, autonomy, and mastery. I help my team figure out their path, guide their journey, and help them reach our shared destination. With this approach, I get smarter cocreated plans and better results. More importantly, my team executes passionately, they have clarity around the path forward, and they are completely bought in to our mission.

THE WRONG WAY TO SCALE A BUSINESS

I began transforming my small-midsize consulting firm to scale past $10 million in revenue with the goal of maintaining service-delivery quality, and client and team member satisfaction. At the time, the enlightened thing to do was to promote from within and hire transitioning service members. So I promoted the five most successful consultants in my business into executive positions and hired a lieutenant colonel, that was just retiring from the Army after twenty-three years of service, all to serve my clients as account executives. I also hired a senior executive from a Fortune 100 company to be my COO.

Combined, their jobs served to care for and support our team members and our clients, and ultimately build the business. The five people that I promoted went from senior program managers overseeing very large projects for my Fortune 100 clients to account executives responsible for my client and team member success. My aversion to salespeople led me to the conclusion that product experts would serve my clients better than a team of sales reps knocking on doors trying to sell to my current and future clients without really understanding their challenges.

Since the team members I promoted had a background in consulting and a deep understanding of our products and services, it seemed sales would be a natural progression. I thought they would be wildly successful because they connected with our vision and the reason we were consulting. They wanted to help people; that's what consultants do.

Within a year and a half, our revenue fell from $10 million to $4.2 million. We went from fifteen Fortune 100 clients to six. We went from fifty-eight billable consultants to thirty. The leadership team I put in place almost put me out of business. And it didn't stop there; 120VC hit rock bottom over the following eighteen months.

And I take complete responsibility. I failed as their leader.

We had mature client-facing products and services but no mature internal policies, procedures, or systems. I promoted six people into executive positions, but none of them had a previous track record of success in these positions. My COO came from a company with large budgets and limited transparency to my small company where every decision was critical and the ramifications were immediate. Running a small company requires a different skill set than a global organization in a Fortune 100. Again, I didn't know it at the time, but I had set them all up to fail.

The hard thing is that I was the leader, and I was supposed to know.

I had employees relying on me, stuck on this journey that I had designed. I asked my leadership team to return to billable positions to help with revenue, and we implemented new strategies to rectify losses. I still believe in the value of promoting from within; now, though, I recommend you don't promote your entire leadership team from within, all at the same time, and bet the company on them. When it comes to organizational change, baby steps are gold.

At this point, I had been a successful boss and a failed leader. The journey to becoming a successful leader took years. Along the way, I experienced major successes and major failures. This book encapsulates the clarity I have today and the discipline I have to show up as a leader 75 percent of the time.

The value created by the team when I "consistently have the patience to lead without the need to solve" is exponential.

Are you wondering why I said I only show up as a leader 75 percent of the time and not 100 percent of the time? Because I am a human being and I am incapable of perfection. Leadership is about change and change is about people. People make decisions emotionally and then rationalize them. So for me, leadership is a journey, like a muscle that needs to be exercised. I won't get it right every time, but I am committed to learning from mistakes and celebrating my wins. I will work to be my best self, the best leader I can be in each moment.

I am grateful for every mistake I have ever made, especially the big ones. I learned the most and the fastest from the big ones, and they were hard and painful. I have felt like a failure, been depressed, been diagnosed with PTSD, and been afraid I didn't have what it took to be a successful leader. After it all, I picked myself up and tried again.

What I learned is simple: talent is a fragile illusion; grit is the secret to sustainable success. With success, I was fooled into believing I was talented. When I hit hard times, I was afraid I had "lost it." The truth is that I'm not particularly talented; my every success came from hard work and not giving up. When I realized this, grit saved me. I learned when something doesn't work, make a change. It's that simple. And I decided to never stop researching, never stop learning, never give up, and never stop changing.

The purpose of this book is to put the techniques that worked for me as a leader in your hands and to do so in a way that works to eliminate, or at least minimize, making any of the mistakes I did. Everything I share has helped me grow a successful management consulting practice. It has helped me succeed for clients like Trader Joe's, Sony Pictures, and DirecTV by completing global enterprise-wide projects and change initiatives as efficiently and effectively as possible—all with near 100 percent adoption on day one *without any authority*. More importantly, it has helped me realize that *It's Never Just Business; It's about People.*

LET'S PRACTICE

My goal for you is to be able to start practicing the concepts you'll learn in the coming pages. As you begin to practice, your results will vary—some will be good, some not so good. Hopefully you will connect with a concept, you will try it, and your journey will begin. You will get results and input; both are informative. The new knowledge will transform you because you will never make a decision without that knowledge. Your decisions will be altered, as will your worldview and the thoughts around the type of leader you want to become.

This book is meant to take you on a journey to develop and refine your leadership skills. Each chapter is intended to give you a "why," frame a situation where a tool or specific technique will help you achieve successful outcomes, and end with an exercise. Then observe your results and build upon them. Let me be clear: implementing these concepts might not go the way you want the first time. In fact, it most likely will not go the way you want. Just don't give up. Leadership is a journey, and you will learn and grow from each attempt.

Let's get started.

PART ONE

LEADERSHIP: IT ISN'T ABOUT YOU

Let me repeat that: leadership isn't about you.

My very first team member and oldest friend, Jake, and I were working through some tough business problems, and he made a suggestion that triggered me.

Me: Is there anything else I could be doing to help you hit your revenue targets?

Jake: You could come to LA and see our clients more.

Me: Dude! That's your job! I've got a job. If we both need to meet with *YOUR* clients so you can hit your revenue target, then there is a problem. There is no way I am doing that!

Jake: Hey man, you don't want to shut me down on this.

I paused and told him he was right. Then I asked him to "say more." And I listened with curiosity and a desire to understand why he believed this was important to the business.

When he challenged me, he was being a good leader to me, something I encourage in all my team members and a concept we will touch on in later chapters. His leadership mirrored a principle I had introduced to him: leadership isn't authority. It isn't a lot of things you may have previously thought. In fact, I am about to shift your view of leadership from an orientation of dominance, control, and self-interest to one of collaboration, intentionality, and service.

CHAPTER ONE

LEADERSHIP VERSUS AUTHORITY

What is authority? Telling others what to do. Why? Because that way you win. You're in charge. You are the top dog. You are the alpha. You get the big paycheck. You're amazing. You're the boss! Every single person on the planet can succeed if they find themselves in a position of authority. But it doesn't scale...

Just because an executive has authority over their employees doesn't mean their employees will follow them. I have seen a CIO's direct reports indirectly fire him by deciding as a team they would not follow him. This particular CIO was left with no way to report on critical activities and no way to influence the outcome of his direct reports' critical endeavors. This quickly became obvious to the CIO's boss and he was fired.

In this situation, the CIO could have used his authority to fire his direct reports before their behavior was noticed, but the business leaders and his boss held them in high esteem. In all cases, this CIO's direct reports did their jobs well for the sake of their success, not for the success of their supposed leader.

The point of sharing this extreme case of mutiny is to illustrate the two distinctly different ways for an executive to influence outcomes: using authority *or leadership*. All executives have positional authority that can be leveraged to achieve results, but they can choose to use their leadership skills instead of their authority to achieve results. Leadership is a choice, and you don't need any positional authority to be a successful leader.

Leadership is exponentially more powerful than authority because it involves choice. When your team members choose to follow you, they are doing so because they either feel positively connected to your vision or because they simply feel connected to you. When this positive connection is in place, your team members will start consciously succeeding for you, their leader.

This subtle shift from their minds to their hearts means that your team members will begin intentionally incorporating the things they believe will ensure your success with their approach to ensuring their success. This will result in much closer alignment between their actions, your vision, and the direction you hope their efforts will take the company.

Connection is the key to leadership, and there are only two ways for human beings to connect with each other: through physical intimacy or by actively listening to each other. Since employing physical intimacy as a leader would be a disaster, I am going to focus on listening.

Fostering connection with your team members requires active listening, versus the more common act of listening to respond. Human nature being what it is, most of us listen to come up with a smart response or to give the right answer. We have a ton of competing demands and are in a hurry to solve the problem. As a leader, if you don't take the time to listen and truly understand the problem or your team members' concerns, your solutions will never be as effective as you would like.

Active listening involves listening to understand how your team members are feeling, how they are thinking, and how they are anchored to a topic. Connection is about feeling understood and feeling cared for. As a leader, when you take the time to really listen—listen as a gift to the person speaking—you will understand them. You will care for them. It's impossible to truly know someone and not feel some connection to them. You will develop a depth of understanding for your team members and it will be evident in how you lead them. The time you spend listening will always be perceived as caring for them, and it will give you the perspective you need to truly *speak* to them...to get through to them...to *lead* them.

Douglas Stone, co-author of *Thanks for the Feedback: The Science and Art of Receiving Feedback Well*, tells us that the receiver is 100 percent in control of whether they receive the feedback constructively or dismiss it as BS. My dad always said that "nobody cares what you think, until they know you care." This is the key to giving constructive feedback as a leader. If your team feels connected to you and feels like you are playing for them, they are more likely to consider your feedback as constructive. Being able to give constructive feedback is critical to influencing outcomes.

In summary, authority is not leadership. And leadership isn't about you; it's about your team. It's about enabling them to succeed and creating velocity for growth by capturing the team's collective IQ, EQ, and their individual *capacity* to drive outcomes.

If you want to be a leader, you're showing up for the team. Otherwise, you want to be a boss, and that's cool! If that's you, here's what I want you to do: right now, leave this book on a bus or a train for someone that understands business is about people.

HIERARCHY OF SUCCESS

The difference between a leader and a tyrant is that a leader works hard for the sake of everyone else, while a tyrant makes others work hard for them.

At 120VC, we commit to leading complex global projects for our clients. Our project leaders need to possess strong leadership skills because they have *no* formal authority.

- They are responsible for ensuring the success of our "clients" by ensuring their projects are successful.
- They are 100 percent responsible for leading the project team members to achieve a transformational outcome. Nobody launches a project because they want their organization to be the same when the project is over.
- They are responsible for moving their projects forward as aggressively as possible, delivering on-time and on-budget, and achieving near 100 percent user adoption on day one.
- All with zero authority.

From my experience, the concept of leadership is widely misunderstood. There is a huge difference between a leader and an authority figure. And there is a huge difference between leadership and management. Our project leaders are never the decision makers, and they completely lack official authority. Our clients decide what they want built, and the project team members decide how it will get built. The project manager's role is to lead them to do this in the most effective and cost-efficient way, essentially enabling the team to achieve the best possible outcome.

Managers have the power to wield the proverbial carrot and stick to manipulate an outcome. Most people that wield the carrot and stick are perceived as exploiting the project team members to ensure their own personal success. Managers can choose to be leaders by inspiring an outcome or can simply wield their authority.

- Inspiring an outcome requires remembering that, as a leader, you are not in charge but that you have a responsibility to those in your charge.
- Leaders don't dictate an outcome; they help their team members focus on what can be done versus what can't be done.
- Leaders help their team members prioritize their workload and run interference when anything threatens to distract them.
- Leaders sincerely care about the success of their team members and focus on solutions, leadership style, coaching, and mentoring in ways that enable their team members' success.

Leaders understand that when their team members

succeed, the project will succeed and they in turn will be successful. People will naturally give their all to the leader they believe cares about their success before their own. People will generally give only the minimal effort required to the authority figure. Authority is the antithesis of leadership and, in my opinion, is an antiquated paradigm. Official authority or not, you can achieve more with strong leadership skills than with authority.

The "Hierarchy of Success" is simple:

1. Work to ensure your stakeholders are as successful as possible. Make sure every decision and every action you take serves this purpose.

2. When your stakeholders are successful, your projects will be a success.

3. In the end, you will be a successful leader that inspires people to reach for *their* potential.

WHY IT'S HARD TO BECOME A LEADER

People see anyone in management or an executive position as a leader. Wrong! Both managers and executives have positional authority, but authority doesn't make someone a leader. Leadership is something you do, a way of being, a way of interacting with the person to your right and the person to your left. Leadership isn't a position; it's an ideology.

Four things make transitioning from doer to leader difficult:

1. **Nobody teaches us that "leadership isn't about the leader."** Effective and even great leadership requires us to put our self-interest second to those we are leading—a task that doesn't come naturally for many of us. In fact, our survival instinct, essentially our ego that never surpasses the emotional maturity of a three-year-old, will always cause us to think of ourselves first. Leadership requires that we catch that impulse before it manifests in an action. Viktor E. Frankl teaches, "Between stimulus and response there is a space. In that space is our power to choose our response. In our response lies our growth and our freedom."

2. **People believe that managers and executives are leaders, but that isn't always the case.** The problem with leadership is that it's super popular! The truth about leadership is that not every situation needs leadership. Great followers, subject-matter experts, managers, and executives are just as critical in a high-functioning organization as leaders. And in high-functioning organizations, there is a time and

place where people in each of these roles will need to step up and demonstrate great leadership.

But, because people are generally wired to pursue their self-interest, they tend to mirror or adopt the behavior of people they perceive as more successful. So labeling the behavior of a boss as "leadership" has established an unsuccessful model for aspiring leaders. Labeling a position of authority as "a leadership position" enables the frontline workers to abdicate any responsibility for learning and exhibiting good leadership skills, and establishes a model of authority rather than a model of leadership for those in management and executive positions. Simon Sinek says, "You're called a leader because you choose to go first into the unknown, not because you're at the top."

3. **We are taught that leaders are superheroes.** Watch any movie or attend a problem-solving meeting in corporate America and you will see managers and executives dictating all of the solutions and saving their staff members from their problems. When there is a critical business problem that needs to be solved, the boss thinks they need to have all the answers. The boss sits at the head of the table and begins assigning tasks until they feel their strategy will mitigate the problem. Then they conclude the meeting and

believe that if their staff executes as directed, they will have saved the day.

Here's the thing. Executives *can't* solve problems for their team members. The executives have the least amount of information and are rarely the subject-matter expert with the chops to identify the best possible solution. And the worst part about treating team members like they need to be rescued is that it implies they are victims of their own incompetence. French philosopher Guillaume Ferrero proposed the "Principle of Least Effort," which postulates that animals, people, and even well-designed machines will naturally choose the path of least resistance or "effort."

If you teach your team that you will rescue them, those that don't want to be rescued will leave and the ones that remain will let you.

4. **Problem solvers get promoted, but what got you here won't get you there.** Managers start off as doers. As a doer they had the best ideas, executed flawlessly, took risks in meetings, and were willing to state the unpopular for the benefit of the organization. They earn their management position by proving themselves, so naturally, when they get their first team, they try to apply that same formula.

STEP #1: INVITE YOUR TEAM TO BE COFOUNDERS

Just like a company starts with a founder, a team is usually founded with the selection of a leader, who then pulls together the team. At first, the team's culture, accomplishments, and reputation are all the product of the founder. However, once the founder selects another team member, they are no longer solely founding the team's outcomes. Each new team member will make decisions and create outcomes that will influence the team's culture, accomplishments, and reputation. As the leader, you can allow them to do this unintentionally, or you can invite them to be intentional about their role as a cofounder.

If you want a high-performing team, it is important to point this concept out to new team members. Let them know that their decisions and outcomes will have a significant impact on each of the other team members, their reputations, and that of the company. Invite them to be cofounders and to be intentional about how their actions shape the culture of your team and impact its outcomes.

LEADERS PLAY FOR THE TEAM

Jake Roig joined my team as employee number one, five years after I started my business. Full disclosure: Jake has been my friend since we were twelve years old. He didn't know a ton about project management when I hired him, but I knew I could count on him to learn quickly, connect with people, and get things done. Turns out I was right. Jake was a successful consultant at 120VC for several years and then wanted to take on a management role for one of our teams. His desire to promote into a management position was partially financial, but he also believed his years of successful experience as an individual contributor would enable him to make a much larger contribution to the business by leading a team of consultants.

So I promoted him into an account executive role where most of the compensation was commission-based. This promotion gave him a ton more responsibility and significantly higher earning potential. All he had to do was grow his existing team and ensure our clients were extremely successful. With this promotion he inherited a team of twenty people across several client accounts.

The result? Over the next twelve months he shrank the team. He set business development goals and then came up with excuses to avoid the work. He continued to find reasons to perform billable work for the client instead of leading his team. He made less money than before and had a negative impact on the business. Don't worry, the story has a happy ending...

I always knew that both Jake and I had an aversion to salespeople. However, it turned out Jake had an aversion to doing anything that looked remotely like sales because he didn't want to be *that guy*.

So for months we went round and round in our weekly one-to-one meeting. We would go over his shrinking numbers and he would make the excuse that he was too busy solving problems with his team members to focus on business development. I would point out that the numbers weren't going to get better if he didn't focus on them. Rinse and repeat. I felt trapped; Jake was a critical member of the team, one of the best program leaders in the business, and he was shrinking my company.

Then one day it dawned on me. I wasn't listening to Jake. I believed his focus was wrong, I was frustrated by his excuses, and I was trying to convince him to focus on the business development because we were losing. I was losing. Like most founders, I had—and continue to have—a deep desire to increase the level of positive impact we could have on the world by growing the company.

I started thinking about Jake. I put myself in his shoes. I immediately realized there was disparity between his words and his actions. Jake knowingly took on a role that required business development to succeed. He was always saying he "wanted to make more money," and business development is where the big money's at. So why wouldn't he do business development work? I knew this was the question I needed to ask him, and I knew I needed to listen to his answer.

I called him and asked if he had some time to talk. I would have planned a face-to-face, but he is in Los Angeles, I am in Seattle, and we needed to work this out ASAP.

I started by framing the conversation with an apology. I acknowledged that I hadn't been listing to him, and that I hadn't been trying to be a good leader, I had been trying to convince him to do something. Short of giving him an ultimatum, I had been acting like a boss. I told him that I had been spending a lot of time thinking about what he said in our one-to-one meetings and that I had a question.

Me: You keep telling me you want to make more money, so I'm trying to reconcile the disparity between your actions and your words.

Jake: What do you mean?

Me: Well, you said you wanted to make more money. So we cocreated a compensation plan that would enable you to achieve that. Then, you appear to be avoiding the work. So, do you really want to make more money? Because your actions communicate you would rather be a billable consultant, and that's totally cool with me! You are phenomenal at it!

Jake: Dude, I really want to make more money.

Me: So help me understand the disparity between your words and your actions.

Jake: I guess I just don't want to come off like a slimy sales guy.

Me: Are you a slimy sales guy?

Jake: Of course not! I care about our clients and it's important to me that they are successful.

Me: I get it. It's pure. It's why you got into consulting and are in this business. It's how we make money as well. Let me ask you this: as your team has decreased in size, have you helped more or fewer people?

Jake: Fewer...

Me: Are you actually taking advantage of any of your clients or trying to trick them into buying things they don't need?

Jake: No! I'm trying to help them!

It was clear to me then: my cofounder had created an obstacle in his mind by telling himself a story that nobody else believed. He was not a slimy sales guy and none of his clients saw him that way. I pointed this out and asked him to let go of the "fake" story or to just commit to being a great consultant.

And he did. He has since grown and expanded his team. It turns out Jake is actually pretty good at sales! And he doesn't have a single client that thinks he's a slimy sales guy.

As a leader, I coached him through this breakthrough. I listened and asked inquisitive questions. I had no idea where the conversation would go, but I saw disparity and I needed to explore it with him.

There were two lessons I took from this situation. If you bring a fight, expect to meet resistance. I was trying to convince him to perform the business development work and this created an enormous amount of cognitive dissonance for Jake. Trying to convince Jake increased the amount of resistance he was feeling toward the business development work.

Second, putting myself in his shoes and really thinking about Jake allowed me to see how I could help. I went into that conversation with no other agenda than to listen and ask questions to understand Jake. I eliminated all potential resistance because I was there to play for Jake. I was also 100 percent prepared to allow Jake to choose. He could have chosen to go back to being a billable consultant and we would have come up with a compensation plan that rewarded him for his expertise. My only goal was to understand so I could help Jake make the best decision for Jake. To help him self-actuate his path toward a shared goal. To grow the business together.

THE ART OF BODY LANGUAGE

My company, 120VC, works with dozens of Fortune 100 companies on huge global projects that pull in multiple vendors. Every project involves a mix of huge egos, and it's our job to get them to work together and see beyond their own personal agendas. The vendor's instinct is to distrust us because the client pays our invoices, and my clients' team members distrust us because they perceive us as outsiders. They wonder who we're going to play for. And we have zero authority. Therefore, part of having credibility and getting people to trust us is the ability to come from an authentic place. When a boss walks into the room, you feel it. When a leader walks into the room, you feel it—but differently.

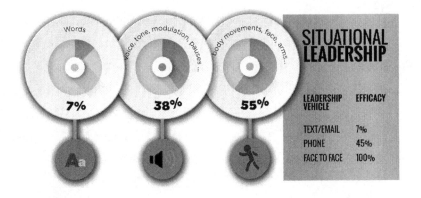

LEADERSHIP VEHICLE	EFFICACY
TEXT/EMAIL	7%
PHONE	45%
FACE TO FACE	100%

When I talk about body language, I need to start by explaining Professor Albert Mehrabian's communication model. The model above depicts the amount of emotion we can pick up from words, tone of voice, and body movement. When it comes to leadership, understanding how people are feeling is important. It's also important for our team members to *see* and *hear* how we are feeling. They want to know if we are being sincere, if we care about them, etc. These emotions are mostly conveyed via tone of voice (38 percent) and body language (55 percent).

On the right side of the situational leadership model above, we expand on the Mehrabian communication model. We took the percentage of emotion conveyed by each communication vehicle and turned that into a model for leadership effectiveness. If you need something simple done, like picking up the copies on the way into the office, an email or text message will suffice. However, if you need to lead a team member through a change in their job description, you will only be able to perceive 45 percent of what they are thinking or feeling over the phone. And in turn, they will only be able to perceive 45 percent of what you are thinking or feeling. Face-to-face will always give you the best chance of effectively leading your stakeholders (up, down, and across). This model can be used to assess a situation and then employ the communication vehicle that will achieve the best results. Remember, the more emotional and stressful the situation and the higher the stakes, the more leadership is necessary.

I've been in a meeting where I've asked the team if everyone agrees with the game plan. If someone says yes while at the same time rolling their eyes, I call them on it. I'll say, "So you mean no?" I usually get a funny reaction the first time I do that to someone, like "What do you mean? I said yes." I usually respond by telling them "Your mouth said yes, but your body said no, and that's okay. Let's just keep talking about it until we are all on the same page. There is a reason you aren't completely comfortable with fully buying in, so let's talk about it."

This summer, my family and I took our twenty-seven-foot Ranger Tug from Seattle halfway up the inner passage to Alaska. Now, a twenty-seven-foot boat isn't exactly small, but mix two adults with a five-year-old and a seven-year-old, add twenty-five days on a twenty-seven-foot boat and you end up with claustrophobia and an amazing adventure! So, two days after getting home from this trip, I was feeling antsy and I asked my wife if she wanted to take the boat to Blake Island for a barbecue lunch. She said "sure," and rolled her eyes. Her tone communicated "I would rather do just about anything else." Her eye roll communicated "I can't even believe you asked me if I wanted to take the boat out."

If I had asked my wife to take the boat out via text message, we would have gone out for the day and I would have ended up with a grumpy family. Since I asked her in person, I was able to hear the contradiction of her words in her tone and we had a great day lying around the house.

ADVOCACY DOES NOT EQUAL LEADERSHIP

Leadership isn't about coming up with the best idea or solution to a problem. Leadership is about helping your team come up with the best ideas. A leader should have ideas, but a leader doesn't shove those ideas down their team's throat. You want to solicit and listen to your team's ideas, not sell them on your own. Remember, if you bring a fight, expect to meet resistance.

Before becoming a manager, early in your career, you had a ton of ideas. You took risks and advocated for your ideas. You solved problems and moved the organization forward.

You were the go-to person, and you were rewarded for coming up with and advocating solutions. Then you got promoted to manager—now what? The shift can be difficult. Your ideas are still valuable; however, you want to enlist the intelligence and help of the people you now lead because that's the value of the team. You now have the luxury of having your team come up with multiple ideas and having a team of very smart people to bounce your ideas off of. Multiple ideas from multiple perspectives makes for better solutions. As an individual contributor you just had yourself.

I succeeded with Jake because I stopped trying to sell him on the idea that his approach was wrong. I instead worked to understand where he was coming from and then move forward together. Ultimately, he came up with the solution. He decided that he could sell without being a slimy sales guy, and even more—he decided that selling was the only way to create additional value for his clients and team members. Leadership was about helping him achieve a shift in perspective.

The biggest mistake a leader can make is advocating his own ideas and perspective and selling team members on why their ideas are wrong. If you do this, your team will stop bringing ideas altogether. Remember, your team isn't wrong simply because an idea conflicts with one of your previously held beliefs. We are predisposed to push back on information that challenges our beliefs, but that doesn't make someone else wrong.

The shift in thinking...you want your team to push back on your ideas and advocate for their own. You want them to feel ownership; that is where the value is created. The idea is to solicit their ideas and share yours and then, with sincerity, explore the possibilities. If they poke holes in your ideas and you explore with an open mind, they will evolve your thought process. Why? Because our perspective blinds us to the possibilities. It's called *Confirmation Bias*.

"Challenge, conflict and critique just rock! We have to look at those things as sources of value creation rather than something to be avoided."

—R. EDWARD FREEMAN

Together you can create things with more value than you would have been able to create alone. Leaders pull the team together and aggregate their value by helping them define *their* roadmap to a shared goal.

THE IMPORTANCE OF LISTENING EFFECTIVELY

In the article "Barriers and Gateways to Communication," written by Carl R. Rogers and F. J. Roethlisberger for the *Harvard Business Review*, the authors discuss the communication barrier as the inability of humans to listen to people inquisitively. We listen to evaluate, so anytime someone shares information, our mind tries to determine if it agrees with each point. When we are asking and answering our own internal thoughts, though, we're not listening or trying to connect with the message—and that's the problem. We are just trying to decide how we want to respond or challenge. Even if you decide you agree, you might start listening again, but you missed the opportunity to understand.

Having a team is the biggest blessing of being a leader, but learning to listen to them is hard. Having a team means you don't have to be the only one ideating and innovating anymore. It's a massive weight off your shoulders. You get to combine IQs, creating exponential value. When you bring a group of intelligent people together with diverse perspectives, you improve on ideas, identify roadblocks, and increase engagement.

Note of caution: I am not talking about building consensus. I am talking about sharing ideas, creating space for other people's solutions, listening and learning from different perspectives, and quickly moving to execution. My formula: Prototype quickly. Test. Fail. Prototype. Test. Fail.

Develop an idea and get it out there. Let everyone challenge it; don't worry about it being perfect or gaining total consensus. Instead, ensure everyone is heard, drive toward an outcome, prototype, and assess the results. If the solution you implemented doesn't work, take it back and prototype again. If you wait for consensus, you're too slow and not as agile as you need to be to win the #RaceToSustain.

GREAT LEADERS MAKE YOU FEEL SAFE

Dwight and Suzanne Frindt, coauthors of *Accelerate: High Leverage Leadership for Today's World*, once shared an amazing concept with me. Consider two circles that overlap in the middle. In one circle, you have people who are born connectors; in the other, you have the challengers. Where they overlap is the leadership zone. Connectors navigate the world by connecting with others. They don't want to disrupt the connection and are uncomfortable saying no. They are conflict-averse. Everyone loves them. And they struggle to help others remain accountable to their commitments. Challengers, who make up only 17 percent of the global population, are wired to say what they feel and drive results. They can be perceived as assholes and therefore aren't effective at motivating or getting great results from others, but they get shit done. To be a great leader, connectors need to move toward the challenger zone, and challengers need to move toward the connector zone. The magic takes place in the middle, the leadership zone. To be a great leader you need to speak the truth candidly and with sensitivity, allowing people to feel safe enough to hear you.

Ed Freeman, a business ethics professor at the Darden School, says, "Challenge, conflict, and critique rock. We have to look at those things as sources of value creation, rather than something to be avoided." Your team has to feel safe and comfortable in order to risk presenting a Big Hairy Audacious Goal (BHAG),[1] challenge your ideas, and on some occasions, do the right thing for the client.

That said...I want to prepare you for this. The first time I asked for this challenge and critique, I severely underprepared for my emotional response. It pissed me off. Even though I had the wisdom to ask for it, the honesty hurt. I got the challengers to critique me in front of the connectors and made it safe and productive, then I was able to get the connectors to challenge. I made them feel safe and allowed them to work together with me on their journey.

I told you up front that leadership wasn't easy, but it's

---

1   Collins, Jim. Good to Great: Why Some Companies Make the Leap and Others Don't. New York: HarperBusiness, 2001.

worth it! You will get used to—and hopefully grow to appreciate—being challenged.

AUTONOMY, MASTERY, AND PURPOSE[2]

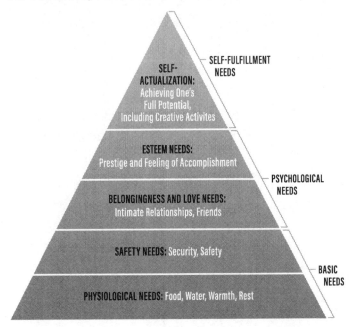

Maslow's Hierarchy of Needs is a theory in psychology proposed by Abraham Maslow in a paper he published in 1943 for the *Psychological Review*. At the bottom of this hierarchy is basic physiological and safety needs. Since we're not living in caves and running from saber-toothed tigers anymore, we need income to feel safe. We need

2   Saul McLeod, "Maslow's Hierarchy of Needs," *Simply Psychology*, May 21, 2018, https://www.simplypsychology.org/maslow.html.

to afford walls, warm clothing, and food. Once we have enough money, our basic needs are met.

Then, we can move up the hierarchy to focus on love, belonging, esteem, and self-actualization. What do these concepts mean? In his book *Drive*, Daniel Pink says that once you take money off the table, people are motivated by autonomy, mastery, and purpose. In relation to leadership, it's important to offer a situation that provides those three elements. To keep your team members happy and engaged in your organization, they need autonomy: which means you can't tell them what to do. They need mastery: which means they need to contribute and add value. They need purpose: a plan and an organization that stands for something they believe in.

At 120VC, our company purpose is as follows:

> That every 120VC team member exemplify the spirit of servant leadership; to be the leaders that all others aspire to be. Because leaders change things; they push the human race forward. Leaders inspire those around them to reach for greatness. And leaders prove that extraordinary leadership does not require official authority, it simply requires that we put the prosperity of our stakeholders first.

What do you get if you take our purpose and synthesize it?

It's simple: leaders serve. In the context of our clients, we provide project portfolio leadership and drive enterprise-wide change efforts that generate breakthrough results. In the context of our team members, we create meaningful jobs that they love and run a company that leverages its successful business platform to drive positive transformational change in the world.

EXERCISE: DEVELOP YOUR LEADERSHIP PRINCIPLES

If you've read this far, you're connecting with the simple premise that leadership isn't about you. You're connecting with the key to unlocking the potential of your team's success, which will in turn enable your success. I'd like to now offer an exercise to determine your leadership values. Determining your leadership values is the first step to uncovering your leadership purpose, and defining your purpose will help you make a lot of really hard decisions.

"That's the hard thing about hard things—there is no formula for dealing with them."

—BEN HOROWITZ

That's why leaders need to define a purpose. To guide them, to help when there is no formula, and to know when they're successful. We can't count on the goalposts to tell us when we're successful, because all we do is move them! When we successfully reach a goal, we set another goal. Success on the journey is about knowing and reflecting on our ability to live our leadership purpose.

DETERMINE YOUR VALUES

Google "list of values," and you'll find a ton of massive lists. Somewhere—use a journal, sheet of paper, or online document—write down every value that resonates with you. Then, take as long as you need to and narrow that list down to your top five values. Put the list away for a week and then take it back out. Do you still feel strongly about those five? If so, you have your top values.

CREATE A PURPOSE STATEMENT

Using the values you listed, create a purpose statement. It needs to be succinct and measurable. Think about the impact you want to have on people. Think about how you want people to describe you and the impact you had on them. When you're done, your purpose statement should feel incredibly meaningful, somewhat aspirational, and achievable.

Your first statement will be messy and will probably change in the next few months, but that's okay. Remember, baby steps are gold.

Once you have your purpose statement written down, share it with people. See how it feels to say it out loud. It will probably feel *very* awkward at first, but it will allow you to get feedback and refine. My leadership purpose statement changed a lot at first; the one I am sharing with you below just stuck! It felt right.

My leadership purpose is "to inspire people to reach for **THEIR** potential."

REFLECT ON YOUR PURPOSE STATEMENT

You've just come up with something beautiful and amazing—something that inspires you. You're probably not living it today, though, because you just came up with it!

To become the leader you want to be, you need to come back to your statement often. Be present and reflect on it at least once a week, if not more. Make an appointment on your calendar for five minutes, ten minutes, or thirty minutes, because the more it gets in front of you, the more likely you'll catch yourself when you're not living up to it. Remember, leadership is about the journey.

CREATE AN IMPROVEMENT GOAL

Different from your purpose statement, an improvement goal is specific to something you want to improve. After spending some time living your leadership purpose, it's time to define an improvement goal.

My current improvement goal is "to consistently have the patience to lead without the need to solve."

When I catch myself jumping in or calling the shots, I'm not only violating who I want to be, I'm also violating my improvement goal.

COMMIT TO A LIFELONG PRACTICE

Do not beat yourself up in the beginning of this journey. If you do, you're more likely to abandon this process of leadership growth—a lifelong practice. We are wired to get it wrong because we are wired to play for ourselves. Leadership is hard. Live in it. Stick to it. Be honest with yourself. When you get something wrong, acknowledge the issue, and recommit to your purpose statement.

CHAPTER TWO

———

WHEN LEADERSHIP IS NECESSARY

Kodak and Blockbuster are dead. Movie theaters are on life support. Barnes & Noble teeters on the brink. These were all market-leading brands that, at some point in recent years, needed to make a shift to connect deeply with their customers' needs—and they didn't. They had executives, but they lacked leadership.

Take Sony. They were the market leader in the electronic audio industry and owned a market-leading record company with their hands on music content. Along comes Apple—a computer company that had to strike deals to get content. Apple wasn't even remotely a competitor until they introduced the iPod. Good-bye Sony.

What happened? What did the company lack? The answer is leadership. Leadership is about taking an organization and its people on a journey. Leadership is more than a willingness to disrupt the status quo; it's about the necessity to constantly innovate. No one hires a leader because they want their organization to be the same when they're done.

Simply put, leadership is about change, and change is about your team's culture. Great leadership is *necessary* when change is imminent or desired. When a brand loses its position as a market leader, it's the clearest indication that its executives have no idea how to inspire change, that its people culture has become rigid, and that its change readiness is dangerously low.

"What's dangerous is not to evolve."

—JEFF BEZOS

LEADERSHIP IS ABOUT CHANGE

I don't know a single executive that feels their teams are driving change fast enough to support the promises being made by their sales and marketing teams. According to DXC, 52 percent of Fortune 500 companies have disappeared since 2000.[3]

---

3 "Digital Transformation Is Racing Ahead and No Industry Is Immune." Harvard Business Review. March 09, 2018. https://hbr.org/sponsored/2017/07/digital-transformation-is-racing-ahead-and-no-industry-is-immune-2

According to Gabor George Burt,[4] it's no longer about satisfying customers, because satisfaction is fleeting. Instead, it is critical to infatuate your customers over and over again. The notion of customer loyalty is outdated. If you aren't constantly introducing new experiences, color lines, flavors, movies, or products, your customers are at risk of becoming infatuated with another brand. People no longer just buy products; they seek experiences. They want to buy products from companies that are constantly creating new experiences for them.

The business environment is where our teams engage, collaborate, and drive outcomes, and that's where change happens. No one is winning the #RaceToSustain customer infatuation if they aren't focused on change. The most significant realization a leader can have is wherever you're at, you are 100 percent optimized for the results you're getting today. If your company has a team of ten people, happy customers, and a successful product, best case, that's how you will continue unless you do something different. It's more likely that without change you will fail to draw new customers and you will fail to keep your current customers infatuated.

Remember this: management is about the work; leadership is about the people. To remain competitive today you need to have a high degree of change readiness and

---

4   Gabor George Bush. "Keeping Customers Continuously Infatuated." Harvard Business Review. April 24, 2017. https://hbr.org/2016/08/keeping-customers-continuously-infatuated.

to have a culture that is always changing, innovating, and learning. To accomplish this, you need great leadership.

MAKE CHANGE A HABIT

Let's say your company wants to increase revenue from $1 million annually to $2 million. To make that happen, you have to change something: add team members or a new product line, market to a new demographic, or change the habits of your existing team. You can't just increase the annual goal, document and publish new policies and procedures, send them to training, cross your fingers, and hope for the best. Goals/policies and procedures are only the blueprints for the new results you seek; getting those results is about shifting your people culture in baby steps through daily and weekly interactions until your team's culture achieves the results outlined by the goals and new policies.

Have you ever spent a ton of time working with your team on a new policy or procedure, only to publish it and become frustrated by the lack of results? Case in point... your team doesn't follow policies and procedures; they follow the culture. We are social animals that conform to the explicit and implicit cultural status quo. If we behave like everyone else, we must be doing a good job. Right?

As a leader it's important to be intentional about driving change, identify small changes or refinements you want to make regularly, and then be intentional about introducing those changes. Share your reason for the changes, tie them to your team's purpose, get their input, and then get their commitment. Then work that change until it is inculcated. Don't introduce a new change until the last change has been mastered. It takes on average twenty-one days to inculcate a new habit. And if you don't monitor the effectiveness of the change you desire as a team, it will get forgotten.

This is where meetings come in...Meetings are where we lead! I have several standing weekly meetings where we focus on different aspects of the business, and once a month we have a board meeting. At the beginning of every meeting, I remind my team that meetings are where we improve and grow. If we conclude a meeting without identifying something we could improve, then we all get a pat on the head and feel like we're doing a good job. And that's great! But if every meeting is like that, we aren't growing. So a really successful meeting is one where we identify gaps for each other, develop a solution, and commit to execution. Every gap we identify for each other prevents a potentially negative future event for a team member, a client, or one of our stakeholders.

LEADERSHIP WINNERS AND LOSERS

In this corner: Amazon. The underdog contender that came out of nowhere.

And in the other corner: Barnes & Noble. The reigning champion and undisputed top dog of the book world.

Jeff Bezos never intended to start an online bookstore. He was a visionary with the goal of leveraging the reach and versatility of the internet to sell products, and he saw books as an easy way to get started. Books are square and light and easy to ship in tidy packages. He ultimately wanted to create an online user experience that met immediate demand, with plans to grow Amazon into an "everything" store.

Bezos started with books to gain initial market share, brand awareness, and get his hands on consumer data. Barnes & Noble, of course, realized they had to compete with the new upstart online retailer, and their reaction was to build a targeted website and online marketplace to sell books.

Where was the change in Barnes & Noble's thought process? The most important idea to recognize here is that when somebody disrupts your business and takes market share, you need to look at the world through their lens. You can't face a competitor disrupting your business by doing the same old thing; in this case, thinking about book sales the way you've always thought about book sales. But that's what Barnes & Noble did. They owned the book supply chain at the time and viewed the internet as just another place to sell product.

It's not just another place to sell product, is it? The critical point to capture with this example is that Barnes & Noble assumed since they were the market leader, they could just continue on the same path. They were very wrong.

Their executives didn't understand that change isn't always about how you do things; it's also about how your team members see things. Barnes & Noble thought they understood the change in the market place, but if that were true, wouldn't they have been the first to sell books online? If they understood the change in the market place, shouldn't they have been able to hold on to their market position?

Barnes & Noble needed a leader that understood that the second you start losing, it's because your people culture has become rigid and your change readiness is no longer where you need it to be to win. To see the change, *your team members need to be willing to change.*

This is where I put a spin on customer obsession. You need to be obsessed with your customers, team members, *and* your competition to be a market leader today. If the leadership at Barnes & Noble had created Amazon accounts and worked to become brand fans like the customers they were losing to Amazon, would they have developed the perspective they needed to truly compete and win?

John Mackey, the founder of Whole Foods, used to visit his competitors' stores regularly. He wasn't there to gloat about the areas where Whole Foods was superior; he was there to fall in love with them. To learn why his competitors' patrons shopped there as opposed to Whole Foods. He did this to see the world through their customers' eyes and be a better competitor.

At 120VC we have a commitment to our competitors posted on our website alongside our commitment to our clients and our core values. It reads:

> The Latin words for compete are *cum petere* and translates "to strive together". We believe that competition helps identify areas that we can improve our business for all of our stakeholders (Team Member, Client, Vendor, Community, Competitors, the Environment and our Shareholders). Therefore, we make the following commitments to our competitors in the hope that together we will elevate the Practices of Leadership, Team Work, and Humanity in the Work Place.

- We will compete with you, never against you.
- We will celebrate when we beat you.
- We will thank you for the opportunity to improve when you beat us.
- We will share our best practices and challenge you to do better.
- We will observe your best practices and improve them.
- We will help you if you ask!

Living up to our client commitment requires a willingness to change. And an acknowledgment by everyone on the team that we are all leaders and we exist as long as we are change-ready.

A GOOD LEADER UNDERSTANDS CULTURE

Solid leadership chops include the ability to change the way people see the world. When you face a competitor or you want your business to perform differently, you need vision. For Barnes & Noble, they should have closely analyzed what Amazon was doing *and* how Amazon viewed the world. Barnes & Noble was the incumbent; they had everything they needed to stay on top. But they didn't. Why? Because they're freaking Barnes & Noble, the (former) incumbent and big dog. They thought they were too big to fail.

An on-the-ball leader would have seen the issue, assessed the company's change-readiness, and said, "We have a new situation we don't like and we have to address it. We're losing market share and we need to shift."

This is very difficult because you've got to get people to *see*. In the business world, it's common for companies to be set in their ways and have a "but this is how we've always done it" mentality. A leader needs to step in and say, "I understand, but we're losing and we can't continue to do things the way we've always done them and expect to win." Barnes & Noble has turned into a general store; they sell toys, books, e-readers, and some stores have a built-in Starbucks. Nothing they've done is innovative.

Barnes & Noble stopped changing and got beat by the competition, and the loss robbed them of their identity. To make matters worse, Amazon is now opening book-stores and giving customers an experience that was previously unavailable, something that should have been easily accomplished by Barnes &. Noble. They didn't because their executives didn't understand that leader-ship is about change.

FALL IN LOVE WITH YOUR COMPETITION

A leader would have tried to understand both the compe-tition and the current customers. What is the experience their customers want? Barnes & Noble could have become Amazon customers themselves. They could have tried to fall in love with Amazon to compete with them, as opposed to feeling hatred for the enemy. Fall in love. That's how you become familiar with a product and the customer experience. That's how you find out what your former customers want and why they are leaving.

The difference between Amazon and Barnes & Noble bookstores is that Amazon brought lessons learned from their online experience to the stores. They developed a tailored customer experience completely focused on what the customer wants, when they want it, and where they want it. "You want a book at one in the morning? Cool. You want us to make book recommendations based on what you previously read? Great. Let us learn about you, and the more we learn about you, the more we can tailor an experience just for you." They did this for millions of people. Consumers became infatuated with the individualized concierge-like experience being all about them.

Personally, I used to enjoy going to bookstores. I could browse books and sit down with coffee and read a little if I wanted to. I also wanted what Amazon gave me. As Barnes & Noble steadily lost market share, their offering became less desirable. Their stores weren't as nice, they didn't offer as many books, and they were closing stores all around me.

Amazon can win opening a bookstore because they've already won. People are familiar and will instinctively say, "Oh, shit. That's an Amazon bookstore. I'm going in there. They have all of my information and know about me. I'll get the same experience I do online." With the purchase of Whole Foods, Amazon captured the brick-and-mortar market and is now dominating both channels.

DRIVING CHANGE

If you want to realize change and drive value, you need to abandon authority and embrace leadership. The terms "change leadership" and "servant leadership" are redundant and cliché because people often think of executives and managers as being in leadership positions. Since there is a high degree of cynicism toward executives and managers in the workplace, the term "leader" has been tarnished. "Change leadership" and "servant leadership" are attempts at recapturing and putting some focus on what a real leader does. Motivational speaker and author Simon Sinek notes that a lot of executives get bonuses for sacrificing their people, rather than taking care of them.

The lack of consumer trust in huge companies and spit-shined CEOs is spot-on. These so-called leaders in positions of power let companies like Circuit City, Blockbuster Video, Sears, and Toys"R"Us die. These giant-box stores have become urban blight, their team members are

unemployed, and their CEOs have moved on to become...
chairman of a board. The solution to the stain on the term
"leader" seems to be the use of the terms "change leader"
and "servant leader," seemingly in the hopes that future
leaders will do a better job if we add a better description
to the term "leader" for guidance.

I call bullshit; these are just terms for the notion of leadership we've long since forgotten. Remember, being in a
position of authority doesn't make you a leader, and just
because you have no authority doesn't mean you can't
choose to be a leader. Leadership is a choice; anyone can
choose to help inspire others to reach for their potential.
Remember the movie about the underdog with no authority that rose to inspire nations? That person didn't have a
business card that said CEO.

THE LAW OF DIFFUSION OF INNOVATIONS

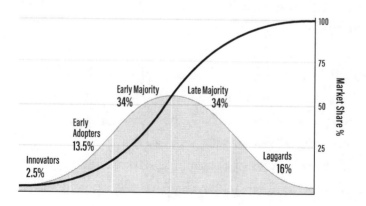

Your goal as a leader is mass adoption of incremental change, and to accomplish that you need to understand the law of diffusion of innovations. This model, or theory, was popularized by Everett Rogers in his book by the same name and discusses how, why, and at what rate new ideas and technology spread.

The diffusion model breaks up society into a bell curve of categories. The first 2.5 percent are the innovators. Early adopters make up the next 13.5 percent, 34 percent is the early majority, another 34 percent is the late majority, and 16 percent are the laggards.

The idea is for innovators to attract early adopters and early adopters to attract early majority. The tipping point is when you reach between 15 and 18 percent of mass market acceptance of a change; you establish a velocity that brings in the next 34 percent. With that in hand, you get another 34 percent. Then, your laggards will either get on board or find a company that is a better fit for them.

What to take away from the law of diffusion of innovations is, first, that change needs to be visible. The early adopters need to see the change has been adopted before they get on board. If you want mass market adoption of a change to your people culture, an idea, or a new product, you have to figure out how to make adoption visible.

Second, the old assumption that the CEO will gather the team for a town hall meeting, postulate on the state of their world, and inspire everyone to get on board is wrong. Expect to get 2.5 percent on board and then expect to work your butt off to get the rest. In other words, being frustrated that people don't just get on board with change is silly. We aren't wired that way. Understanding the law of diffusion of innovations allows us to make a much healthier assumption. We can assume that people won't just get on board with the change, that we will have to help them by being great leaders and by making adoption visible.

GET CHANGE-READY

Change requires time. It requires a buildup. Your innovators need to get excited first, so you have to start building adoption long before you need a change to occur. If you are deploying an enterprise change—especially a technology change—you're doing it to capitalize on an opportunity you see in the marketplace, and it will take time to build. Technology doesn't innovate; it enables people to innovate by maximizing their potential. If you can't get near 100 percent adoption of the new technology on day one, you are at risk of missing the opportunity after spending the time and money to deploy the new tech.

Get the people you need to adopt involved long before the product launch. Allow the innovators to get excited and share their excitement, work with the early adopters to build champions for the change and share their excitement, and so on, all the way through each category of adopters. Get them all sold long before the product launch and let them wait in anticipation. Then you might get near 100 percent adoption on day one.

Never forget, your competition sets the pace. Because you never know what your competition is going to do, your goal as a leader is to prepare your organization to drive change as fast as necessary by introducing small changes constantly. If your competition is slow, you're in great shape. If a company shows up on the scene with afterburners blazing and you aren't change-ready, you're dead. BlackBerry products provide a great example of this dynamic. The only way you have infinite time to dial in your product is if you don't have any competition. In the beginning, BlackBerry only had Nokia competing with them, and both companies were innovating at the same pace. Then the iPhone and Android came along, and BlackBerry got killed.

The example of BlackBerry's failure at the hands of Apple comes back to leadership. A leader drives change in an organization at an appropriate pace, while recognizing the impact of that change. When the need for change moves into the imminent stage and you need to adapt quickly, you need your team to be change-ready. If change isn't a constant part of your culture, don't assume people are going to be excited to jump on board; you will lose every time.

Your biggest advantage is to understand that leadership is about change, change is about people, and people adopt change according to the law of diffusion of innovations. Armed with that knowledge, you can drive a cultural shift much quicker than if you assume a role of authority.

WHAT LEADERSHIP LOOKS LIKE

Leadership is encouraging people to participate so they feel like what is happening is in service to them, not being done to them. In particular, where there is fear, people need engagement.

We've recognized that 2.5 percent will get on board with proposed changes, and everyone else is likely wondering how it will affect them. It's a common misconception that people don't like change—or, worse, fear it. I don't think that people fear change. I find that people are afraid of the potential loss associated with change. And to make matters worse, most people are terrified by the unknown. When presented with a change, people start wondering how it might affect them negatively. And without evidence to the contrary, most people leap to the worst possible conclusion.

Some people in management feel it's best to keep company plans quiet. These managers fear transparency because they don't trust their employees to act in the best interest of the company if they perceive they will be negatively impacted. The downside of this strategy is that no one is going to get behind a change strategy if they don't know how it is going to impact them. Human nature is to assume the worst. Some will drag their feet, some will look for another job, and others will work directly against the change initiative.

The best way to get from the first 2.5 percent to the next 13.5—from innovators to early adopters—is to sit down with everyone and be transparent about what you know and what you don't know. What has been decided and what you still need to figure out. The project and change managers assigned to develop and execute a plan need to understand it's not as simple as defining the project and identifying tasks. They also need to talk with key players and ask about their feelings, thoughts, and concerns, then incorporate solutions for those concerns in your change strategy.

It's important to encourage everyone to share their concerns and fears and address them as quickly as possible. If you just tell key players it's going to be fine, they won't believe you. This is a surefire way to create a mass exodus from your company and completely hamstring your ability to move quickly to implement the change. Instead, identify the plan for change with them and the impact it will have on them, especially those that will be negatively affected by the change.

Work to eliminate any resistance associated with the unknown. People don't resist change—instead, they fear the potential loss associated with change. When people have clarity, even if the outcome is not ideal, they have choice. And...clarity makes seeking their fortunes elsewhere the greater unknown. Remember, choice overcomes fear of the unknown and helps people to engage in the process.

TREAT YOUR VENDORS LIKE TEAM MEMBERS

The business world often forgets that the vendors they employ are also project stakeholders. If you have purchased a product and their implementation services, or if you are relying on them for their expertise, then their failures impact the project end date, cost, and product quality—just like the failures of the internal team members.

I have encountered executives that chose to utilize their leadership skills over their authority with their internal team members. In every one of these instances, their team members thrived and were considered to be top performers. I have also observed (ironically) some of those same executives forsake their leadership skills and rely solely on their authority when it came to their vendors.

This approach seems to imply that vendors are on their own to succeed or fail and the only responsibility these executives take for the vendor's success is to hold the vendor accountable, but with no responsibility to help the vendor succeed. The great irony here is that vendors are always working at a disadvantage.

Vendors are experts of their domain but not the client's domain. They start off unfamiliar with their client's environment, politics, and processes, and they don't have any beneficial relationships. That means vendors and their personnel need more assistance to succeed than the internal team members because their failures have the exact same impact on project success as the failures of internal team members.

My point is this: it is critical to treat vendors and their personnel as you would internal team members to cultivate their success. Vendors are funded, have broad industry relationships, and their teams are vast. When things go south on a project, the vendor that feels a deep connection with their client leader and the project team will pull off the majority of your Hail Mary plays!

EXERCISE: BEGIN ACTIVE LISTENING

Active listening techniques are critical to connecting with your team members, developing trust, and understanding how to lead them. More importantly, active listening gives you the credibility to shift a team member if you disagree with them, and the ability to have your coaching construed as constructive. The most important takeaway: truly listening to understand builds connection, and with connection comes trust. If you want your team members to lean in and play for the team, they have to trust you are playing for them.

ASK QUESTIONS

The next time one of your team members escalates a problem, suggests a change for the organization, or brings a new idea, ask them questions. Start by asking them "why" to understand the impacts. "Why is this a problem?" or "Why should we make this change?" Even if the "why" is immediately obvious to you, make sure they have thought it through. Remember, leadership isn't about you. Then ask how they think the team should approach the change. Ask them to come up with the solution while you use active listening to help them develop the most effective roadmap to a shared team goal.

Periodically, while your team member is talking, interrupt and paraphrase back your understanding of what they shared. This will allow them to clarify points that aren't in alignment with their thought process and improve the quality of the picture that is developing in your head. Paraphrasing also communicates the points that you understood accurately and will earn you the credibility to challenge their vision, if necessary, for the sake of a better outcome.

Here is the active-listening formula:

- Find opportunities to paraphrase your understanding of the "*who, what, why, when,* and *how*" of the vision. Don't be afraid to learn that you didn't see it correctly. If your team member clarifies, you are making progress!
- Ask "Why?" a lot! Ask questions to understand the reason, history, and benefits behind the "who, what, when, and how."
- Ask open-ended questions—questions that require more than a yes or no answer. Get them to describe instead of just getting an answer.
- Challenge assumptions and become the architect. Think beyond the description given and see if you can think of something important to the vision that hasn't been addressed. Then ask questions like "Have you considered...?" or "What if this happens...?"

The exercise of active listening will help you develop a

deep and comprehensive understanding of their vision and will force your team member to think more deeply about their solution/approach than they had previously. This exercise almost always causes their initial vision to evolve into something crisper and more beneficial for the team. This evolution of thought through active listening is what leaders do. We lead people. We help them see things differently for their benefit. We lead them to better conclusions and ultimately help them reach for *their* potential. Leaders don't tell people what to do; we help them see what to do.

DON'T STAY SILENT

Some people see active listening as simply sitting and really focusing on what someone is saying with an occasional "Uh huh, I see." That's actually passive listening! If you're not asking questions, you're not trying to understand, and you'll miss something. It's much better to stay engaged and ask questions throughout, creating a two-way dialogue and establishing credibility for your understanding of what your team member is sharing. Just don't take over the conversation and make it about you!

CHAPTER THREE

LEADERSHIP REQUIRES PREPARATION

"HOOAH!"

Al Pacino made that one word the most recognizable line in the movie *Scent of a Woman,* belting it out with conviction during a college class assembly looking to hang Chris O'Donnell's character, Charlie, out to dry. Pacino unleashes a spontaneous, powerful rant against college brass for tearing the honor from Charlie when the school is supposed to be about developing leaders.

Mel Gibson delivered a similarly spontaneous inspiring message to his fellow warriors in *Braveheart* before leading them into a bloody battle. Both movies, naturally, had great writers portraying leaders in epic leadership moments when characters have all the right words and always know what to do. Let's face it: do you really want to see a movie where the leaders get it wrong all the time?

Hollywood paints leaders as a one-in-a-million enigma—they're just born that way and can roll into any situation and know what to do and say. The fact is that winging legendary speeches is not reality. The popular adage "Leaders are born, not made" might hold some truth or not, but even born leaders don't wing it every time. If they do, they're not getting it right. To get it right, you have to prepare and consider what's ahead of you, what you need to accomplish, whom you need to pull it together, and how you can serve them. Preparation makes you more efficient, strategic, patient, and aware of assumptions and the necessity of learning rather than dictating.

You might feel like you have to wing it sometimes but, personally, I'd rather not. When I find myself in a situation where I have to wing it, it might be because I feel there's no opportunity to put things on pause and save it for another meeting. But the truth is, most things can wait. Saying, "I need some time to think about this before we get into it" shows maturity and intentionality. Remember, great leadership is most necessary when change is imminent or desired, a.k.a. when there's a problem. And great leadership requires preparation.

It's a scientific fact that when our heart rates exceed 110 beats per minute, we are subject to our bodies' fight or flight response. In fight or flight, two of our brain centers shut down and we are reduced to the emotional maturity of an eight-year-old.

If something's not going well, the leader needs to pull the teams together and help them work through a course of action. Bad news stresses everyone out. Sometimes you need a moment to digest. Take a pause, take a deep breath, and center yourself. Then schedule a meeting where you can show up prepared and focused.

Taking the time to prepare lets me think about the people involved, look closely at the situation, and separate the facts from my assumptions. Our perception of a situation is a combination of what we observe (facts) and the assumptions we make about those observations. I find it helpful to write down what I have actually observed or what I know to be fact versus conjecture. Then I can work with my team to develop a solution with a clear-eyed assessment of the situation.

PREPARATION'S ROLE IN LEADERSHIP

It's a brain thing.

More than a few people out there claim they aren't emotional, but they don't realize emotions are a built-in, chemically driven feature. Our brain interprets something, releases a chemical, and our bodies translate that into emotions or feelings.

The brain is a wildly complex and mysterious place. Beyond the left brain/right brain processes, the neocortex hosts our logic, reason, and speech center. Then there's the limbic system, the "old brain." This is the place where we feel—what many people call the subconscious. Interestingly, the limbic system is also where our decisions are made. The way we're wired in that decision-making part of the brain is also the emotional brain, and our neocortex only rationalizes decisions made by our subconscious.

Many leadership books talk about being intentional and present and driving decisions from the top down—or from your logic center. That takes years of work, and it's not what this book is about. Whether you consider yourself an emotional person or not, keep reading, because your emotions drive your decisions 99 percent of the time. It's all in the science.

The first step in preparation is considering how you feel about the situation. You have an opinion and a feeling about the situation. You have a positive or negative feeling associated with the issue at hand: you may not like it, it may not be your favorite thing, and so on. But it doesn't matter. It's not about you.

PLAYING FOR THE TEAM

Before you can put yourself aside and play for your team, you have to identify where you're at, where you begin, and where you end. If you're unhappy about something, take a few minutes to breathe deeply and reset. You can't be stressed and calm at the same time, and deep breathing resets our nervous system and allows us to return to calm. This goes for both extremes. Let's say you're all fired up about a specific business opportunity. You'll go into the meeting with a spring in your step and, because of confirmation bias, you'll only hear information that confirms your assessment of the opportunity, and you'll steer the team toward that choice. On the other hand, if you feel negative about a situation, you'll infect others with those same emotions. Either way, if you are in the way, you can't play for the team.

CHANNEL YOUR INNER EMPATH

Helping others get the best results helps your business get the best results. For me, it starts with a thought. The more I think about my team members, the more I empathize with them. First, I identify where I'm at emotionally, acknowledge it, put it aside, and think about how the situation might impact them. Do they see it as a good situation or an opportunity? Do they see something negative or just extra work they won't be excited about? More importantly, what role will they want to play in relation to their level of expertise?

I prepare myself for the fact that they are going to show up as human beings; some will be excited, others won't. I prepare myself to allow either to be perfectly okay, regardless of what is on the line. If I suspect someone is going to show up with a negative perspective, I won't be caught off guard and react negatively. I can then make it safe and productive for them to share their views. Encouraging both the positive and negative views as a means to work toward the best possible outcome helps people feel productive and actually increases their positivity. In fact, making it safe and encouraging all perspectives releases serotonin in the brains of those that are sharing. Serotonin increases our positivity and happiness level in the moment, opens the learning centers in our brain, and increases the productivity of our brain by 30 percent.

If I've put substantial thought into the situation and the individuals, I can bring a great deal of value to the meeting. More importantly, I can turn something they might see as negative into a positive opportunity for the company. Everything we need to succeed is already there; it's all in how we choose to perceive it.

BE AWARE OF THE COLLECTIVE HEADSPACE

Being conscious of your own headspace goes a long way in engaging productively with people. I often refer to the DiSC behavioral assessment when looking at the dynamics between people. The DiSC is a long-standing work that quantifies different psychological preferences in how people perceive the world around them and subsequently make decisions on those observations. If you and your team can assess their types, it will help you navigate interactions in the long run. You'll understand how each individual sees, hears, and feels in response to particular situations. More important, you can understand their worldview and their values. For example, a team member that scores high in dominance (D) is going to relate to personal power, risk-taking, control, and respect, whereas someone that scores high in influence is going to relate to achievement, ambition, success, and status. Understanding my worldview and each of theirs allows me to transcend my personal characteristics and preferences to relate to theirs.

Understanding my worldview allows me to be aware of my triggers and empathize with how my team members may be perceiving our current situation. Remember, leadership is not about power or authority, and generally speaking (whether you like it or not), you're the most powerful person in the room, and others will gravitate to whatever you're feeling. In very rare cases, someone else might exude something seriously significant to overpower the leader's vibe, but, for the most part, you are the piper. It's important to acknowledge that whatever emotion you bring to a meeting will prevail.

And last...Shawn Achor, an expert in positive psychology, teaches us that our brains at positive are 30 percent more effective than at negative, neutral, or stressed. If you bring optimism to a meeting, you might also get innovation. If you bring pessimism or negativity to a meeting, go ahead and uninvite productivity.

FAILSAFE STRATEGIES FOR PREPARING TO LEAD

What is the best way to prepare to address critical problems or communicate new directives to your team? I use a technique that works well for establishing a steady-state mindset well before a meeting takes place. If I have to address a company issue, I first schedule a meeting with myself. I take fifteen quiet minutes, write down the issue and desired outcome, and let myself mentally engage so I am completely at ease with the details and potential solutions. It's my job as a leader to ensure we reach a positive outcome and move forward. No problem gets better with age; the longer it sits there, the worse it gets. The same goes for the story people tell themselves about the problem, catastrophizing it to the point of hysteria.

In my premeeting, I write down and underline the facts that are observable about the situation. I detail what I know and outline the assumptions I am making. I have learned that the second I hear about a situation, my limbic system takes the observable facts and fills in the gaps with assumptions to produce a complete story. Our brains do this to protect us from harm and to allow us to react immediately. Our limbic system doesn't bother with logic; its job is to keep us alive. Point being...it's human nature for us to jump to conclusions. Knowing this, I like to spend time unraveling the story before a meeting so I can be an effective leader.

Once I have briefly outlined the situation, the impact, the observable facts, and my assumptions, I start thinking about the story each of my team members might be telling themselves. Then I remind myself that the worst possible thing that could happen almost never happens and that once again we have been presented with an opportunity to learn and grow: an opportunity to be masterful problem solvers and to move the company forward.

With my notes at hand, I simultaneously think about the people on the team and remind myself not to expect them to see the situation the way I do. It's not often that a group shows up really excited about a problem. It takes a very optimistic person to see a problem as an opportunity; when we do that, the situation almost always turns out better than it was before. For example, if I have a critical problem in respect to a client and approach it as an opportunity to do a better job, improve the client relationship, and learn and improve as an organization, I almost always do!

DON'T TREAT ANYTHING LIKE A PROBLEM

Treating an issue like an irritating problem you just want to make go away sets the stage for negativity and blame.

"Blame is the discharging of discomfort and pain. It has an inverse relationship with accountability."

—BRENÉ BROWN

When preparing to lead a team through a problem-solving discussion, I have three objectives: solve the immediate problem, learn what we could have done to achieve a better outcome, and put that knowledge to work in my organization to ensure we don't make the same mistake twice. To prepare myself to accomplish those objectives, I typically assume that the team will be defensive and then remind myself that that's a human reaction so I don't get triggered. I know as we explore the problem, they might be reluctant to be forthright about their roles, discuss their mistakes, or consider what could have been done differently, in a public space. However, if we can't openly analyze the situation, we will struggle to come up with a solution, we won't learn anything, and we are likely to repeat the mistake.

Remember, the idea of addressing a critical problem isn't to find someone to blame; it's to identify a solution and a lesson we can use to improve. In order to reach this objective, people need to own their part of the problem and communicate openly to the group—something that's hard to do, even for the best of us.

ENCOURAGE TRANSPARENCY

Go into a problem knowing you need to encourage people to open up. Openly applaud those on the team that are willing to be vulnerable about their role in creating the problem in front of other team members. Make it more than safe; give them rock-star status! Make vulnerability sexy! Make vulnerability the next rock star.

As I said, it's common to face silence or only murmured responses in a group setting, and you need to prepare yourself to walk into a room with people you know are likely to be disappointed or reluctant to talk. Their nature might be to protect themselves and cover things up, and it requires efficient emotional preparation to face this situation in a productive way. Be prepared to encourage transparency and vulnerability by asking for it and then rewarding it publicly. If you shoot the messenger, you just fucked innovation.

EASE BACK ON THE THROTTLE

Most people in executive positions are drivers, but as a leader it's best to slow it down. If you walk into a problem-solving meeting expecting people to be fired up, ready to hit the problem head-on, and prepared to be fully transparent, you have failed to reflect on every problem-solving meeting you have ever participated in. Regardless of how many times your team attends a problem-solving meeting, that just ain't gonna happen; that's why we need leaders! The other problem with making that assumption is that you are preparing yourself to get triggered and immediately start calling the shots, telling everyone what needs to be done to solve the problem. And that would end badly.

With a reluctant team, it's easy to fall back on the instinct to just solve the problem yourself. And doing that would be like giving someone driving directions to any location without first asking them their current location.

In your mind, the team is in Los Angeles and you start telling them how to get to San Diego. They're nodding because they just want the problem to go away and you have a solid track record of saving the day. The meeting ends and they all jump to action. The next day, they show up to give you an update and the results are not even close to what you expected. Now you've lost a day, the problem isn't solved, and you have no choice but to ask how they got here. What you learn is that they were not in Los Angeles; they were in San Francisco. You assumed you were giving them directions to get to San Diego from Los Angeles; they assumed you knew they were in San Francisco.

The point of this ridiculous analogy is twofold: to remind you that this has actually happened to you and to remind you *why* leaders don't solve problems for their teams. Instead, you help them self-actualize a roadmap to a shared goal that you are super comfortable with. Leaders help their teams identify solutions by asking questions and challenging assumptions until a plan materializes that everyone is happy with. When your team leaves the room, you are clear on their next steps and so are they. The results you hope for are inevitable.

Remind yourself to listen, be patient, don't solve, and engage them in the game. Reward transparency; continue to peel the onion until your team is fully on board and has an aggressive solution.

THE 2 × 2 PRIORITIZATION MATRIX

A few years ago, I was fortunate enough to get nominated to attend the Integral Leadership Program at the Stagen Leadership Academy. This program is focused on helping transform executives into leaders and teaches us how to focus our energy to become 100 percent intentional about everything we do. One of their tools is called the 2 × 2 prioritization matrix. It's both simple and an incredibly effective way to prioritize your initiatives, communicate them to your team, and enable your team to self-organize around them. Got agile?

Every week I make it a priority to prepare for the following week. If I were to wait until I walked into the office Monday morning to determine my plan for the week, I would get swept up in the whirlwind. I would end up reactive and running around, caught up in a serotonin haze, solving problems. Yes, I'd be working, but would I be growing my company? Would I be addressing problems I know need attention to ensure we are moving forward and achieving our goals?

No. Absolutely not. I would just be busy.

2 x 2 Prioritization Matrix

High	Selectively Invest		Do First / Drive Daily
	1		1
	2		2
	3		3
	4		4
	5		5
	6		6
Value			
	Ignore / Delay		Work In
	1		1
	2		2
	3		3
	4		4
	5		5
	6		6
Low			
	High	Effort / Cost	Low

The matrix consists of four quadrants. The horizontal scale shows level of effort and cost, decreasing as you move left to right. Vertically, there is a value scale, with the lower value at the bottom. The upper right quadrant includes things of low effort and cost but high value to the organization. We call this section "Do First/Drive Daily." Moving to the upper left, we have "Selectively Invest." These tasks are high effort and cost, and also high value, such as large projects and organizational initiatives. The lower right quadrant is low effort and low value. These are tasks I'll "Work In" to my weekly routine. The last quadrant is high effort and cost, low value. These are "Ignore/Delay."

For your 2 × 2 to be effective, you need to revisit it every week. I create mine at the beginning of the year and review every Thursday. As mentioned earlier, I have several weekly reoccurring meetings that focus on different aspects of the business. I review my "Do First/ Drive Daily" items and then update the agendas in these meetings for the coming week to ensure I am prepared to "Do First/Drive Daily."

The items in the "Selectively Invest" category are generally projects that will run for a period of time and then complete. To address these, I set up weekly reoccurring meetings to make sure we are making regular/steady progress on these initiatives. Every week I review the 2 × 2 and backlogs for these initiatives and then update the agendas for the coming week.

DAILY STATUS REPORT

Quick side note: if you are an agile shop, we treat these meetings like weekly sprint planning meetings. Each initiative has a vision, roadmap, and backlog, and we all publish daily status reports (DSRs) to each other in lieu of a daily stand-up. A DSR is a single "barely sufficient" status from my team members focused on accomplishments and next steps for all of their initiatives, and it's way more efficient than hosting a daily stand-up for each initiative. If we did that, we would spend all of our time in meetings. It only takes five minutes for each of us to read each other's DSRs, comment, and prioritize our day. The DSR format is simple, and we set them up as an email signature so we don't have to recreate them every day. We just click the insert tab, select signatures, and select DSR. You can find DSR instructions on my LinkedIn profile. If for some reason you can't access them, send me a message; I am happy to share.

Then I move on to my "Work In" category. This category works as you would expect. I look at the remaining windows on my calendar for the coming week and block time or schedule meetings to address my "Work In" items.

"Ignore/Delay" is my favorite category. It allows me to keep track of the things I think are good ideas but require no action. Anything that sits in any of the other categories for more than a month with no action, because I can't find time to get to it, gets moved to "Ignore/Delay." This approach helps me stay realistic about what we can accomplish and eliminates the "everything is a number one priority" mentality. It enables me to make consistent progress on the things I believe are a priority.

When I am done, my calendar for the following week is full. It's full of things I consider a priority to accomplishing our immediate objectives that tie to our current year's plans. If something comes up during the following week that seems like a priority, I am forced to weigh its importance against what is already on my calendar. If it's critical, I can move something scheduled into the next week. This process forces me to weigh seemingly immediate needs against my priorities.

Most of corporate America feels compelled to be committed to everything, and they run around in high-speed circles trying to juggle it all while not making much progress on anything. If you adopt and follow the 2 × 2 process that I outlined above, you will get shit done and those items you accomplish will be the ones you consider your highest priorities.

ALIGNING THE MATRIX AND COMPANY VISION

One of the great things about the 2 × 2 matrix is its alignment with our company vision, which we call the Painted Picture (with credit to Cameron Herold). The Painted Picture is a visual representation of where we're going this year and beyond. From a twelve-month perspective, we know what we are focused on this year; from that, I develop the matrix. I share that with my direct reports so they are clear on our immediate priorities, and then they create their own 2 × 2s that align with mine and all of our priorities are in sync.

EXERCISE: PREPARE TO LEAD BY IDENTIFYING THE STORIES

Leading by separating the story I am telling myself about a situation from the observable facts is the quickest way for me and my team to get clarity and drive toward a solution. As mentioned earlier, much of what we perceive about a situation is an interpretation of the facts rather than a clear-eyed assessment of the situation that separates facts from our assumptions.

This exercise starts by identifying a problem that needs to be addressed with your team. It could be related to performance, culture, attitude, and so on.

OUTLINE THE SITUATION

Take fifteen minutes to write down the situation. Describe the problem. Make a list of the observable facts, then a second list that outlines your assumptions. Your assumptions are your instincts about the situation based on your experience. These are distinctly different than the facts that you have observed and know to be true.

Once you have your list of facts and your list of assumptions, write down how the situation makes you feel. Think about the desired outcome. Run through the meeting in your head, and prepare yourself for the stories your team might be telling themselves and how they might feel. Prepare to show up for them.

VISUALIZE THE PRESENTATION

Imagine presenting the situation to your team by saying, "Here's the problem. Here are what I know to be facts. Here are the assumptions I'm making. How do you think we should solve this?"

PRESENT IT TO THE TEAM

Take your prepared problem to the meeting and present it as above. Ask them to develop a solution. Be prepared to use active listening to help your team members work through the possible solutions and remind yourself not to solve the problem for them. Note that you don't have to share the part about how the situation makes you feel; that's just part of preparation. Simply acknowledge it but don't take it to the meeting. Fold it up and leave it in your back pocket.

RECOGNIZE FIGHT OR FLIGHT

If you've been the leader who always gives the solution to the team, that team is not going to know how to go through this exercise, and they will need your help to get started. Tell them, "I need to empower you. You are intelligent, capable, and talented, and I think our business would be stronger if I started engaging you as a team to develop solutions."

If you're the leader who is constantly engaging your team for solutions, good for you. In that case, the story exercise is probably just a different format to get to clarity quickly. It's an exercise where you are taking the time to prepare and you're also taking the time to get clear on your story. If you can kick off a meeting knowing what parts of your story are assumptions, you can work with your team to eliminate them. For example, you might need to ask a customer a question before you can come up with a solution. Assumptions will drive or shape the solution. If you focus on the facts and work to eliminate or substantiate assumptions, you're going to be able to respond quickly and effectively.

The story exercise helps move the needle by engaging your team and driving toward clarity. Be realistic and confident in their ability to solve problems. Trust is a powerful motivator.

CHAPTER FOUR

LEADERS NEED LEADERSHIP

Leadership isn't about processes and procedures; it's about creating a culture of listeners, collaborators, challengers, and decision makers. Leadership is about enabling your team to self-actualize by giving them a voice and engaging their creativity. Great leaders are *the* proverbial sounding board. By creating a culture of leaders, team members can provide the same support to each other and their leadership. But be careful—since we communicate to lead, speaking carelessly equals leading carelessly, and that has consequences.

Just because you employed active listening, asked questions, and paraphrased doesn't make it okay to say, "Now that I understand what you're talking about, I think that's a fucking stupid idea and we're going to go another direction." That approach makes everything you did up to that point a complete waste of time because you just made it unsafe to express views and opinions. Much of this work is combined with considerate messaging. Say what needs to be said when it needs to be said, and *attempt to say it in the way it needs to be heard*.

Now, I am sure you already knew that careless messaging is bad for business. This word of caution is more about inviting your team members to be leaders. As their trust builds, so will their comfort level, and if they are going to be good leaders to you, they need to understand and practice considerate messaging as well. Candor is critical to getting to the root of a challenge quickly, but it doesn't mean we can be inconsiderate.

At 120VC we believe we communicate to lead. Period. If an interaction leads to confusion or shuts someone down, or a leader doesn't get the results they were expecting, that's not poor communication; it's ineffective leadership. Sure, you could make the case that it's also poor communication, but then you would work to improve your communication instead of focusing on improving your leadership. It's important to focus on what needs improvement, and leadership is about outcomes. If you aren't getting the outcomes you need, it's not about communication; it's about leadership.

Encouraging everyone on the team to be a leader is good for the team, and it opens the door to let others' expertise show the leader where growth and change can occur. I recommend that you invite your team on this leadership journey with you. If you choose not to invite them, don't be surprised if you encounter carelessness in the way they offer feedback. Sadly, people seem to be most careless with those people they feel safest with. It's not unusual for people to speak to family members in a way they would never think to speak to friends. Adopting the mindset of a leader in all aspects of your life will allow you to inspire everyone in your circle of influence by remembering one simple thing: we communicate to lead.

TURN FOLLOWERS INTO LEADERS

If leadership is so great for self-actualizing everyone on the team, what about the leaders themselves? How can they participate and benefit? You're a leader and a team member with a stake in the game. You're leading first, and ultimately, you might have to make a final decision. If everyone agrees on a solution, it's easy. Either way, you invest a lot of time and effort to help your team self-actuate a roadmap to a shared goal.

When we share our opinion with the team, we can benefit from the same leadership support we give them; wouldn't it be great if they practiced active listening and challenged our assumptions to ensure we have a 360-degree view of the situation? Ironically, I am painting a picture of a leader that sounds more like a follower, and that's the point. Regardless of your role, if you want a high-performing team, there will be a time when each member needs to be a great follower and each member needs to be a great leader. I make a habit of pointing out in public when someone on my team has shown me great leadership.

Recently, I was in a finance meeting with my controller, Christeen Hershey, and the rest of my leadership team. I committed to completing a task and Christeen asked me when I planned to complete it. Her question prompted me to put a placeholder on my calendar to complete my commitment the following week. In that simple question Christeen helped me be more organized and better prepared to be accountable to my commitment. I acknowledged to everyone in the meeting that in that simple question Christeen showed me great leadership, and I thanked her.

Simon Sinek says that "you are called a leader because you choose to go first into the unknown, not because you are on top."

A leader will always be the leader and the first to go into the unknown. At the same time, a leader needs their team to show up for them as well; otherwise, there is no team. A high-performing team recognizes good leadership, and everyone shows up as a leader when needed.

TIME TO GROW

Events in my company's past offer a great example of this leadership dynamic. Here's a story of how I broke my own rules and caught myself just in time for a good outcome. In a meeting with Jake, the general manager of our southern California operations, we talked about the progress we were making to address the concern that our business had plateaued over the past two years and it was negatively affecting the morale of our team. We had spent the past ten years focused on hiring highly talented team members with a focus on aptitude and cultural fit. And we treated them like the "talent," which is to say they are the stars of the show we call 120VC.

The challenge with talented team members is they need to feel challenged. Once you take money off the table by paying top-of-market salaries, mastery is at the top of the list of factors that motivate us in the workplace.

Because the business had plateaued we weren't creating new opportunities for our team members to grow. We realized our top talent wasn't feeling motivated, so we decided we needed to focus on growing the business as much as we focused on doing a great job for our clients.

To do that, we had to first decide how to develop a strong sales team. It's a tricky conundrum: if you're not growing, you can only help a finite number of people and you won't retain your team members; if you want to grow, you have to be good at what you're good at *and* be great at sales and marketing.

At the beginning of our journey to develop a sales team we accidentally hired sales reps that, over a period of a couple of months, only reinforced our aversion to salespeople. We really struggled to find sales executives that connected with our core value to "care about people," as opposed to simply caring about closing any deal that would put commission in their pocket.

In parallel, we realized we needed to modernize our recruiting process because our ability to hire to keep up with client demand was very low. Clients wanted to work with us, but we struggled to find and hire talented people. This forced our clients to work with other management consulting firms and ultimately impacted client satisfaction. To address this, we started looking for a talent acquisition system and committed to hiring a talent acquisition leader once we had a sales rep on board with a pipeline of new business.

The plan was to grow our footprint in Southern California and expand into the Seattle market. In the middle of a debate on which location to focus on hiring a sales representative for, Jake had an idea.

Jake: I've been thinking about this, and I really think that we should hire a talent acquisition leader before we focus on hiring a sales rep.

I'm thinking, we had previously agreed on sales reps first, had lived through several bad hires, and I had just recently engaged a retained search firm to find us a sales rep. I had just written the check! And now Jake wants to do something different? I balked.

Me: No. We agreed that we're going to hire a sales rep. I just wrote a check to a retained search firm and spent hours with them to clarify our needs and create targeted search criteria. I don't want to talk about this.

I shut it down but then caught myself. We were on a video conference, and I threw my hands up in the air.

Me: Hey man, you know what? You obviously think this is a good idea. So let's talk about it.

Jake watched me catch myself and he did the same thing.

Jake: No, no, no. Let's talk about why you think it's a bad idea.

We both shifted into good-leader mode to listen to each other—a great example of how I successfully taught my team how to mirror good leadership techniques. And how I often catch myself when I am failing to be the leader I aspire to be.

Jake began by pulling out a spreadsheet to walk me through the numbers. Of the number of opportunities we had had in the last year, talent acquisition was only able to find team members to hire to fulfill 45 percent of the opportunities. That meant 55 percent of the time we had to apologize to clients and lost the business to another firm. If we had been able to fill even 80 percent of that, the revenue and profit would have increased significantly and been more than enough to cover the cost of a talent acquisition leader and several additional sales reps.

The data opposed our original thinking, which was that additional sales reps would bring in additional clients and create more opportunities to hire team members. His point was that we were not fully taking advantage of the existing pipeline, and if we were to add a sales rep, they might become frustrated with talent acquisition's ability to hire in order to keep up with their sales. It was a great point and one that was not even on my radar. Had I not taken the time to hear him out, I would have moved forward with a suboptimal plan.

This story is a cautionary tale for aspiring leaders. You're going to make mistakes as you transition from a boss to a leader. However, if I had been the boss and not a leader, we would have hired an additional sales rep, and I would have lost out on the opportunity to improve my talent acquisition team and grow the company. We achieved a better outcome because I caught myself being a "shot caller," shifted to leader, and listened. Jake felt heard and appreciated, and I encouraged him to continue to bring ideas to the table and to continue challenging my thoughts for the sake of value creation. Jake was a good leader to me that day.

ARE YOU CONVINCED YET?

Convincing someone doesn't put you on the same page. In fact, convincing can sabotage success. Convincing means selling someone on why your opinion is right. You talk past someone and try to win them over.

In business, anytime you're not open or you draw a hard line, you've basically created a situation where the other person will either argue or just shut down and stop offering solutions. If you bring a fight, you can expect to meet resistance. Even passive resistance.

TAKE OFF YOUR DECIDER HAT

With a team of listeners, collaborators, challengers, and decision makers in place, I can take off my decider hat and wear the "challenge appropriately" hat. Frankly, this is so much easier than coming up with all of the answers all of the time. And when you have several talented people willing to get vulnerable and really tear the issue down until it's naked, you get better results. Instead of being the guy calling all the shots or being "the boss," I get to ask "why? what if? have you considered?" If I can stump someone, we research further and come back to it. I even get to offer up ideas, but I'm not the only one. To avoid "follow the leader" I wait to share my ideas until I have created a frenzy of problem solvers.

I can come to meetings and tell a story about a problem, and we go through what we know, separating the facts from the assumptions. Then I ask the team to come up with solutions. Ultimately, as they offer ideas, I help them create momentum.

THE RULE OF TEN

Years ago, I attended a skills workshop for CEOs billed as "The Power of Team Member Engagement." Not so ironically, the best way to teach a CEO is to allow them to experience the message and to draw their own conclusions, so the facilitator split us up into groups of four. He gave each group a card with a description of a problem and asked us to come up with ten possible solutions. He didn't tell us the purpose of the exercise; he just gave us the assignment with a ten-minute deadline and started the clock. I am sure that you can guess we had four possible solutions immediately because CEOs have all the answers! The fifth and sixth solutions took a little longer, but seven through ten took most of our time. Each subsequent solution took longer and required more thought and discussion from the group.

At the end of the ten minutes, we were told to stop. The instructor asked us to raise our hands if we had come up with ten solutions. Most of the groups had. Then the instructor gave us two minutes to decide as a group which of the solutions was the best. At the end of the two minutes, the instructor asked us to raise our hands if the best solution was one of the first five, and nobody raised their hands.

Forcing us to come up with more than the first few obvious solutions required us to think harder and collaborate more with the other members of the group. In every group, the best solution fell between sixth and tenth on the list.

In that moment, the "Rule of Ten" was born. When my team or one of our project teams is working to define the best possible solution to a critical business problem, we employ the rule of ten. The rule of ten requires us to come up with ten viable solutions for a problem and then decide on the best one. Coming up with ten solutions will ensure the following:

- There is no question that we have done our diligence.
- We will execute the selected solution with confidence.
- We have increased the potential for success on the first try.

Why this works: studies show that, when developing solutions, the first few come quickly and are based on our past experiences. This is called "anchoring" or "focalism." The problem with basing solutions for a current problem on a past problem without doing your diligence is that the situation is never exactly the same.

TEAM MEMBERS NEED A VOICE

As a leader, it's imperative to realize the benefit of giving team members a voice, a role in shaping the future of their organization. In order to do that, people need to know they can speak up.

One of the common threads of the brands we love, known as affinity brands, is that all of their employees are empowered to make decisions, all the way down to frontline workers. The reason you'll pay six dollars for a cup of coffee at Starbucks isn't because their coffee is any better than the shop down the street; it's because the team members are happy and they're empowered to help you. If you walk into a Starbucks and ask for a pepperoni pizza, the barista won't just gloss over and tell you they don't serve pizza. Instead, they will say something like "We don't serve pizza here, but two blocks down is the best New York slice in town." They are engaged, and they want to help. If you don't believe me...try it!

Southwest Airlines is another great example. Their flight attendants tell jokes to passengers. Nobody in the corporate office told them they had to do that, but someone thought it would be fun, tried it, and the passengers loved it. Word spread among employees, and pretty soon it went viral.

Starbucks and Southwest Airlines know how to fully empower team members to serve their core values and goals, and you can do the same with your team. Encourage them to identify their own masterful approach to achieving a shared goal and you'll come away with innovative solutions and happy team members. When you look at affinity brands—more are Costco, Google, Starbucks, Chipotle, Whole Foods, Amazon.com—they all have empowered teams.

Instead of the ideas being driven top-down by one boss

or one corporate executive, a flight attendant decided to start telling jokes. A blend of empowered teams and receptive management led to innovation and epic consumer experience.

FROM DICTATOR TO LEADER

I'm the first to admit I tended to stubbornly defend my ideas. I'd think, *It's my company; we're going to do it this way. I'm not really interested in anybody's ideas.* Naturally, people don't react optimally to that approach. They might do what you ask, but they're not going to grow or learn. Ultimately, you'll find yourself needing to save the day over and over again.

As I worked to develop my company, be a good leader, and get better results, I reflected on how changes in my behavior had changed my relationships with my team. I realized on the days that I was patient and empathetic or felt like I wanted to work on something with them and wasn't so focused on the result, everything came together. Now, I pause before I speak; instead of simply evaluating their proposals, I ask questions to understand.

Most of the time, when you tell somebody precisely what to do and how to do it, they're simply going to take notes and go do it. Then you are going to cross your fingers and hope yours was the best solution. On the other hand, you could frame and then ask a question: "We need to get better results in talent acquisition. Do you have any ideas?" By asking a question, you've engaged their mind and curiosity, and they're going to begin problem-solving. By the time you're done with the discussion, they may have already thrown out several ideas, and more ideas lead to better results.

We don't just communicate to lead; we listen to lead. I started becoming intentional about my communication in that I now understand that what and how I communicate is predictive of the outcomes I can expect.

SHIFTING FROM ADVOCACY TO INQUIRY

The secret formula for effective leadership is to adopt a beginner's mind and develop a deep understanding of your team's decisions. If they come to you and ask how you want them to do something, you have to be able to ask how *they'd* do it.

If you're going into a meeting to solve a business problem, you will absolutely have already thought of some way to make the problem go away. That's how you became an executive, right? You were the person who had the ideas and would solve the problems. In your role as a leader, it's important to take the time to allow your team to come up with a solution and to remain open to the possibilities. If, during your meeting preparation, you don't acknowledge you're going to want to provide the solution, you're missing the most important part of the exercise: to check "you" at the door and go into the meeting playing for your team.

It's also important to understand that, while you're encouraging your team to come up with solutions, you're not going to like everything they come up with; that's just part of the critical-thinking process. If someone presents an idea you're not keen on, don't say, "That's not the best idea," get impatient, and tell them what to do! That's advocating and labeling. Instead, redirect them to another potential solution by restating your understanding of the solution being proposed, and then reframe the desired outcome. Say something like "Well, if our goal is...how does your solution get us there?" It's a chance to refocus their attention, and it requires you to have the patience not to solve the problem for them. Remember, if you are dictating outcomes, you are managing. If you help them get clarity, you are leading.

EXERCISE: RELINQUISH THE DECIDER HAT

I think the thing that helped me the most on my leadership journey was that I came up with a leadership improvement goal for myself. Leadership is helping my team members self-actuate their own path to a shared goal. It means that I'm helping them come up with solutions to solve problems and achieve our business goals. When they're successful, I'm successful.

My improvement goal is **to be a consistent leader by having the patience to lead without the need to solve**.

This might be a little tough at first because, if you haven't been this leader, your team is used to you solving problems for them, so there will be an adjustment period. Over time, though, they'll start to understand. They'll get excited. They'll feel empowered. You're giving them a new platform to develop their mastery—to determine their own destiny in respect to driving business.

The next time someone asks what you think they should do, stop yourself from immediately providing a solution. Instead, ask, "If I weren't here, what would you do?" or "Come back when you've made a decision and we can talk about it."

These days, I just laugh and say, "You know I'm not going to tell you what to do, right?"

Regardless of how you solicit a solution from them, do not answer their question. Have them explain the situation and the outcome they desire. Have them separate the facts from their assumptions about the situation. Ask them what they would do if they didn't have to worry about failure. Then practice active listening until they have committed to an action and a completion date. Always get "what" by "when" or you don't have a commitment.

If you were historically the decider, there is a possibility that you have some folks on your team that don't have the desire or aptitude to come up with their own solutions. The exercise of relinquishing your decider hat will empower those with the attitude and aptitude to lead, engage, build, and grow. It will also show you who on your team doesn't. Treat those that don't with kindness and empathy, and help them find a good manager. If you allow them to stay on your team, high performance is not achievable. You and the others will end up carrying them, and that will lead to resentment. The healthiest thing to do is to help them find a home where they can thrive, inside or outside of your company.

CHAPTER FIVE

MEETINGS ARE WHERE WE LEAD

A leader doesn't change anything alone. If I'm standing in a room talking to the wall, nobody's following. Meetings are where we lead! Whether it's a one-to-one meeting, a chance hallway conversation, or a formal meeting with a large group, a meeting is your stage, your leadership forum.

Meetings are also where the team plays on the field at the same time. Meetings are game time and where we move the ball as a team. We meet as a team to gain agreement in the form of decisions, create and commit to solutions to solve problems, or identify and assign tasks that create velocity toward the completion of a business objective.

Between meetings is the time for solo activities, like working on your pitch, improving your batting performance in the cage, or lifting heavy weights to improve your hustle. When you are on the field with your team, you need to be ready to lead. Like leadership, productive meetings require preparation.

A MEETING'S ROLE IN LEADERSHIP AND CHANGE

Meetings are fundamental in providing a safe place to build trust and honesty. They are where we model leadership, establish commitments, and help people be accountable—all publicly.

There is an interesting mechanism in our brains called anchoring.

Let's say I have a one-on-one meeting with a team member. In that meeting, my team member commits to an action and a completion date. That commitment gets anchored to me in their memory. When they leave my office, they have every intention to execute that commitment, then they head to their next meeting, then on to the next...By the end of the day, they have completely forgotten about the commitment they made to me in the wake of their follow-on meetings. Two days later, they see me in the hallway and think, *Shit, that's right! I told him I would complete something by close of business today.* Seeing me in the hallway triggered their memory anchor. It's this dynamic that makes public commitments more powerful than private commitments. People often believe that public commitments are more powerful because of the shame factor, but in reality, the more people you can anchor a commitment to, the more likely you are to remember to keep that commitment. You get a reminder each time you see the faces of the other meeting participants, talk to them, or meet with them in a day.

Then there is the law of diffusion of innovations. This book focuses on leadership, change, velocity toward a goal, people, and adoption, so it's easy to see that a leader's job is to shepherd us through a constant state of fluctuation and change. In any given moment our commitment to these changes is also fluctuating, and we need to see the commitments or adoption of others to continue to reinforce our own commitment.

Meetings are where this happens. If you prepare to lead in your meetings, you will consistently drive productive outcomes. Consistently productive meetings reinforce a culture of productive meetings that generate agreements in the form of decisions, good commitments to solutions, and accountability to assigned tasks that create velocity. When team members feel productive, they go from meeting to meeting energized, their brains at positive functioning 30 percent better than at negative, neutral, or stressed. When they see their team members accountably completing their commitments, a culture of accountability is born and your performance increases.

Adoption of change needs to be visible. It starts by mastering meetings, modeling good habits, and achieving the planned outcomes. If you and your team exist in a culture of meetings that fail to achieve outcomes, then your company is going nowhere fast. There is a difference between busy and productive. You can assess your company's change-readiness and agility by the number of meetings that accomplish their planned outcomes versus the number that don't. If you survey your team members and find out that the majority of them feel that most meetings they attend are a waste of time, you are not change-ready and you aren't winning the #RaceTo-Sustain customer infatuation.

MOVING FROM CONFLICT-ADVERSE

If your team is conflict-averse—uncomfortable talking about any problems or possible dysfunction and refusing to have hard conversations—you have to find a way to move past that.

First of all, if you're not having tough conversations, you're not innovating anything. You're probably not growing quickly, and you're definitely not change-ready. You can't move very quickly as a team, especially in today's business climate where there's no business leader who feels like they're driving change in their organization fast enough to keep up. You can't get there unless you have a team that is truly comfortable having tough conversations, a team fully willing to challenge, create conflict, and critique for the sake of value creation.

You can create such a team in baby steps during meetings. You can do it together. Each time someone takes a risk and is rewarded, it leads to a productive conversation—which, in turn, helps the team move forward. In the next meeting, someone else will have the courage to do the same; it's a snowball of constant productivity. To get there, simply introduce the concept of challenge, conflict, and critique as necessary for value creation. Then encourage team members to lean on that principle when they feel they need to say something that might be perceived as negative. They can declare "I'm feeling a bit nervous about it, but I feel like I need to use the challenge, conflict, and critique card. I'm only saying this for the benefit of the team..."

THE TIME FOR ONE-TO-ONE MEETINGS

One-to-one meetings do serve a purpose: they allow trust to be built between the leader and an individual. They let people feel safe talking with me as a leader, and they can serve as a primer for feeling comfortable talking to the group at large. You may also need a one-to-one to challenge someone's performance or to address potential resistance to the direction the team is headed. Pull them aside to explore the obstacles and avoid calling them out in a public meeting. One-to-one meetings are incredibly important to build trust, provide evaluation, and coach someone. They are not sufficient to steer a team toward a common goal or drive any substantial culture changes. That work must be done publicly as a team.

THE REAL PURPOSE OF AN AGENDA

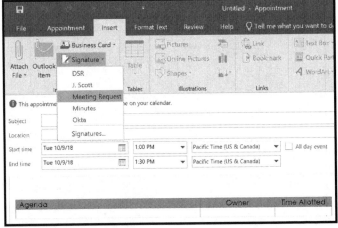

The exercise of preparing a meeting agenda prepares you to lead and to achieve the outcomes you need to maintain velocity. Given the relationship between effective meetings and an organization's ability to efficiently achieve desired outcomes, anyone that schedules and chairs meetings at 120VC is required to attend "The Art of Leading Meetings" training and obtain their "Meeting Leader Certificate." This may sound silly, but given the role that meetings play in an organization, I am shocked that most companies allow anyone with an email address and calendar to schedule and conduct meetings.

In addition to the training, we require that all meeting chairs prepare and publish agendas within the meeting invite sent out to attendees. Again, we use the signatures feature in Outlook to format the meeting invite to include an agenda in the body.

The exercise of developing an agenda in advance of the meeting consists of the following:

- Clearly and concisely identify the meeting accomplishments necessary to achieve the desired outcomes (agreements, solution identification, task assignments).
- Identify only the team members with the expertise and authority to define and agree to next steps. Do not invite anyone that is not critical to accomplishing your agenda items. The staff at *Harvard Business Review* wrote an article where they ask, "How many people should you actually invite? There are no hard and fast rules, but in principle, a small meeting is best to actu-

ally decide or accomplish something; a medium-sized meeting is ideal for brainstorming; and for communicating and rallying, you can go large."[5]

- Model out the duration of each agenda item by thinking through the questions that will need exploration and the associated team members' personalities (connector, challenger, etc.). Determining the duration of agenda items is critical to determining an adequate meeting duration. Your agenda items may require several meetings to accomplish, and you don't want to find this out after waiting for and conducting your meeting.

When developing your agenda items, identify the meeting outcomes that will most successfully move your initiative closer to completion or create velocity toward a business objective. Think of agenda items as future accomplishments. Good agenda items are clear, concise, and measurable. Another way to formulate agenda items is to think of them as outcomes.

One of the biggest obstacles to moving a business objective toward completion as aggressively as possible is meeting lead times. In most Fortune 100 companies, people's calendars fill up weeks in advance. It is not

---

unusual for people to be double- or triple-booked weeks in advance. When planning a meeting, finding a time slot when all the necessary attendees are free at the same time is very difficult and almost never happens the same week you send the meeting invite out. The time between sending the invite out and the first available time slot for all attendees is called "Meeting Lead Time."

If, after developing the agenda, you find that your meeting duration is longer than thirty minutes to an hour, don't arbitrarily decrease your meeting duration. This will ensure you fail to complete each of your intended accomplishments, and you will have to schedule a follow-up meeting. Because of the meeting lead time, it could be weeks before that next meeting can take place. Instead, split the agenda items into several meetings and schedule immediately. This will ensure you are able to facilitate the meetings necessary to move your initiative forward as soon as possible. Proper agenda-item duration planning will help you determine the duration needed for your meetings. This activity helps you avoid the pitfalls associated with meeting lead time and helps to ensure that you frequently accomplish what you intended in your meetings.

PREPARATION BREEDS PRODUCTIVITY

People in corporate America often wake up in the morning, look at their calendar, and see every single time slot throughout the day isn't just booked with one meeting—it's booked with four. Why? They receive multiple meeting invites three weeks in advance, and they don't know who's going to cancel, who's going to show up, or what's going to move around. What do they do, then? They accept them all.

Such meeting inconsistency is the very reason people get visibly, physically angry when they feel like they went to a meeting that didn't accomplish anything. When I'm speaking, training, or teaching, I ask the class, "Raise your hand if you've ever been to a meeting where you felt like your time was wasted." Everybody raises their hand. Then I'll say, "Okay, keep your hands up if that made you angry or feel frustrated," Nobody lowers their hand. I end with a final inquiry: "Lower your hand if you weren't getting paid to be in the meeting." Everybody's hand stays up. They were all getting paid to be in a meeting where they felt their time was wasted, and they were still frustrated—proving money isn't enough to keep people engaged and thriving at work. It reiterates the 2013 *State of the American Workplace* Gallup report that identifies what motivates people in the workplace. Spoiler alert: it's not money. The poll actually found that once people make enough money, they are motivated by autonomy, mastery, and purpose.

The bottom line? If you prepare to lead, model out your

durations, schedule meetings considering lead time, and ensure your meetings are productive; when someone looks at their calendar with a choice to attend your meeting or someone else's, they will come to yours. Why? Because you allow them to feel productive.

HOW TO RUN GOOD MEETINGS

Once your agenda is done and you've scheduled the meeting, it's time to run the actual meeting. I feel it's very important to have operating principles in a meeting that people can refer back and be accountable to. In our meetings, the first thing we do is rotate throughout the group and read aloud the 120VC Meeting Guidelines. No matter how close you are as a team, if you work through the tough stuff and someone gets triggered, it's easier to step back and take a breath with these guidelines in place.

TEN RULES OF ENGAGEMENT FOR MEETINGS

1. Meetings are to move forward. Participate as a founder by stating **possibilities** and **not obstacles**.

    Lead with the possibilities. People tend to fixate on why we *can't* as opposed to trying to figure out how we can. Remind everyone at the start of the meeting to seek possibilities and not fixate on the obstacles. When people lead with the obstacles anyway, I like to write them on a whiteboard under the title "Obstacles." To drive the point of rule #1, I wait until they are finished and then erase the title that says "Obstacles" and retitle them "Solutions Needed."

2. Participate by stating **facts** so we can make **good decisions**. We can't make good decisions based on opinion or speculation alone.

   Participate by stating facts and identifying the assumptions. It's amazing how often I see meetings degenerate into spinning around people's opinions. If you listen closely for the speculation, it's easy to spot opportunities to move the meeting forward by committing to the facts. Speculation is fine as long as it enables progress.

3. **Listen** intently to the question being asked and be sure to **respond** to the question **in context**.

   There is nothing more frustrating than watching someone take the time to frame a thoughtful, productive question to the group and have someone respond to the question completely out of context. It leaves me wondering at what point the responding team member stopped listening because they had already come up with an answer? Our tendency to listen to respond instead of listening to understand is a challenge to our ability to make progress as a team.

4. **Respond to** statements or direction given by explaining how you **understand**.

    This habit is key to achieving agility and the outcomes we need as a team. If we developed the habit of paraphrasing our understanding, we would never have any misunderstandings. We would clear them up in real time and our execution would always be on target.

5. **Offer counter**-direction or alternate **proposals** only **after** executing #4.

    This guideline is very powerful when disagreeing or proposing an alternative to anyone. If we don't restate their position, they will assume we didn't understand and attempt to reassert their point of view. This could feel argumentative and provoke us to jump to defend our point of view.

    If we first restate, they know we understood and are better prepared to listen to our point of view. Learning this was one of my all-time favorite light bulb moments. It is the first step to helping others overcome their confirmation bias and a critical step in conflict resolution. If you step into a conflict with someone and want to get out productively, start by paraphrasing your understanding of their point of view before responding. The implied empathy alone will quickly calm the situation.

6. If you have a concern, **participate** by asking **questions** in the **pursuit of possibilities**.

It has become popular in corporate America to voice our concern. It's almost like people listen to find a flaw so they can announce their concern and save the day, except voicing a concern without a nod toward a potential solution is just a roadblock to progress. First, concerns generally arise due to our confirmation bias. And our confirmation bias assumes that we are right and the other person is wrong. So, announcing a concern communicates that the person speaking is ignorant and we have all the answers. See what just happened? You started a fight.

Instead, ask questions assuming you are the one that doesn't understand. See if you can find the possibilities in what the speaker is saying. My go-to question is, "What if you do that and this happens? What would you do then?" If you need to frame a question by stating your perception, state your perception as one of many possible perceptions, as opposed to the obvious truth. Remember, if you bring a fight, expect to meet resistance.

7. When addressing a mistake, our purpose is to create an approach to a **better future outcome**. Focus the conversation on what we will do next time. Meetings are about the future.

> *"Blame is the discharging of discomfort and pain, and has an inverse relationship with accountability."*
>
> —BRENÉ BROWN

8. When a team member begins defending themselves, the entire team will take a break and reset. No one needs to defend themselves, **we are safe**.

    No matter how safe we make it, sometimes it's hard for someone not to end up defending themselves when we are at the root of a problem the team is trying to solve. The second that happens, we are no longer making progress and the person defending themselves has switched from problem solver to fight or flight. It's best to acknowledge that what they are feeling is natural and that everyone should take a few minutes to reset. I think it's also a good idea to thank them for their willingness to be vulnerable and remind them they are safe.

9. **Participate** actively and **as a founder**. Multitasking marginalizes your contribution to the team's effort.

When you invite people to a meeting it's because you need their participation. Not just to weigh in on their area of expertise, but to participate critically in all aspects of the decision-making. A founder is rarely the master of all domains, and founders listen critically to everyone's opinion in an attempt to find the best way forward. Founders are completely bought in and don't have a golden parachute. Imagine if everyone in the meeting were participating as a founder, playing both team member and leadership roles. Solutions would be bulletproof. Multitasking sends a clear message to other participants that you have no interest in playing for the team.

10. **Take** individual **responsibility** for the outcome of each meeting. Don't blame others.

   Members of high-performing sports teams don't blame a loss on a single team member. They each watch the game films and attempt to identify ways they could have played better, supported their teammates, and ultimately contributed to a win. They own their personal contribution to the team's failure. When a meeting fails to create value, a high-performing team spends time evaluating their personal contribution to the outcome of the meeting instead of casting judgment on their teammates.

GET COMMITTED

Commitments come from meetings, and public commitments are a large part of a successful approach to leadership. I follow a framework developed by Donald Sull and Charles Spinosa.[6] In their article, "Promise-Based Management," they offer a framework consisting of five characteristics of a good promise: public, active, voluntary, explicit, mission-based. One of my team members, Michael, turned this into an acronym—PAVEM—and we use it to foster good commitments.

PUBLIC

If you make a commitment in public, you're anchoring that to the whole team. Literally any interaction with the people that were present when you made the commitment will help remind you to get it done. In a world of competing priorities and more work to do than is possible to keep track of, having multiple memory anchors to help remind us to be accountable to our commitments is very useful.

ACTIVE

An active commitment starts by asking questions to understand what we are being asked to do, and even

---

6   Donald Spinosa and Charles Sull. "Promise-Based Management: The Essence of Execution." Harvard Business Review. August 01, 2014. https://hbr.org/2007/04/promise-based-management-the-essence-of-execution.

negotiating if necessary. If someone is requesting that you deliver something on a day you are already committed to work on something else, it's totally appropriate to negotiate the completion date to ensure you can remain accountable to previous commitments.

The second aspect of an active commitment is restating your understanding of what you are committing to. What you restate is predictive of the result the requester should expect. If what you restate isn't in alignment with what they are hoping to get, they can clarify in that moment. When you get the nod of approval that what you restated is in fact what they are looking for, you both have clarity. You can confidently execute knowing you will deliver as expected and the requester will have confidence in the result they are going to get.

VOLUNTARY

If saying no isn't an option, then you can't count on "yes." I don't mean that people should refuse a request without an explanation. I mean that they need to be able to say, "I can't work on that right now; is there someone else?" If your team doesn't feel like they can say no, they will say yes to everything. When people say yes to everything, "yes" becomes meaningless very quickly because they will fail to deliver on every "yes." The first step to creating a culture of accountability is making "no" a positive.

EXPLICIT

When you set expectations, be clear about the basics: who, what, why, when, and where. I've seen executives say to a group, "You know what? We need some fresh ideas. I need some fresh ideas by the next meeting for our approach to marketing this new product." Everybody just nods their heads, and they all think somebody else is going to take care of it. Then the next meeting comes along and no one has done anything. This ties into another 120VC best practice: never assign a task to multiple people; tasks have a single owner.

MISSION-BASED

As often as possible, explain why the task is needed. In my world, it's nearly impossible to get around because, most of the time, the people defining the work are subject-matter experts. We talk about the "why" so they can come up with the "what" and the "how." Ultimately, if the person understands why they're doing something and see the value it's meant to achieve, they can problem-solve their way through it when they run into obstacles. Conversely, if they don't understand why they're doing it, they're going to have to come back to you—an inefficient circle. The "why" gives them the ability to problem-solve, and it also ties to our desire for purpose. If we know why we're doing something, we're much more motivated than if we see it as work for work's sake.

GETTING TO YES THROUGH THE POWER OF NO

There are four perfectly acceptable responses to a request for commitment: yes, no, promise to promise, and counteroffer. Naturally, we love it when someone says yes, and you should celebrate when someone has the courage to say no. Making progress requires predictable outcomes so you can spread the initiatives efficiently across players. When someone says yes because they don't feel comfortable saying no, you will not get the expected outcome. Promise to promise means "Let me look at what I have going, and I'll get back to you in an hour." Counteroffers simply means "I'm already committed to another project. Can I get it to you Friday morning instead?"

THE POSITIVE POWER OF NO

William Ury wrote a book called *The Power of a Positive No*. He presents a great deal of research on how people in general are uncomfortable saying no. They feel saying no could negatively impact their relationship or reputation, so a lot of people just won't say it. The irony is that after failing to deliver on your yes, it catches up with you. It's shortsighted and hurts the relationship later. Yet, human nature being what it is, almost everybody struggles with saying no.

When I told my wife, Colleen, that I'd learned most people are uncomfortable saying no, she said, "Not you!"

We laughed. After reading the book, I had a heightened awareness for the common aversion to saying no. The next time I found myself in a situation where I needed to say no, I realized I didn't feel great about it. Although completely willing, I became aware of my own aversion to potentially hurting the relationship by saying no.

This helped me empathize with those that would rather get into a car accident than tell someone no. I realized it was my job to make this safe and help shift people's perception of no. I needed to make "no" a positive at 120VC and on the projects with our clients. If people aren't comfortable saying no, you can't count on "yes." As project leaders, we need to be able to count on "yes" or we have zero predictability in our outcomes. We need to cultivate cultures of accountability, and the only way to do this is to make "no" a positive.

I presented this information to my team and students. I explained creating awareness around this is critical; if we say yes when we really mean no, it inevitably hurts the relationship and the business. If you're committed, "no" is a great answer. If you say yes and don't deliver, that's bad. We needed to make "no" more than safe, we needed to make "no" a positive.

A CASE STUDY ON NO

Several years ago I asked my leadership team to begin working with our consultants to start forecasting their hours out one week in the future. I told them I wanted to get a handle on cash flow. In my mind, I asked for this baby step with the goal of getting everyone comfortable with forecasting their future hours. Then, I planned to ask them to increment to ninety days and ultimately to six months.

They committed to getting the forecasts implemented three weeks from that day. Five weeks from that day, we were on a leadership call, and I realized there was still no forecast in front of me. I said, "Guys, you promised to get forecasting in place two weeks ago. It's not done, and nobody said anything to me." Total silence fell.

I didn't yell and scream, but I was mad. I was triggered, so I acted like a boss.

"This is bullshit," I said. "All of you committed to getting this done, right? You blew it off and nobody told me. I'm going to get off the phone and give you ten minutes to figure this out. When I get back on the phone, you're going to make a commitment to me, and you're going to keep it."

When I came back, they made a commitment to me, and

we moved on. The day after that meeting, I felt insecure about the commitment. I wondered, since they blew me off the first time, how would I know they weren't going to do it a second time? This mental space isn't a good one for a leader to be in, and it's not the relationship I want to have with my leadership team. I need to be able to trust that they will deliver on their commitments.

So, after about a day of wrestling with this uncomfortable feeling, I called Jake. I told him that I couldn't stop thinking about what had happened and that I was still feeling insecure about their commitment. I started asking questions, and I listened to the answers. "What happened? Where was the breakdown? I'm not feeling confident that I'm going to get the results that I asked for, even the second time, so talk to me about why it didn't happen."

He explained to me that they had all talked about it several times, and they didn't see the value in forecasting a single week. They knew any sort of change is disruptive to the team, there's resistance, it would require work, and they already felt like they were juggling a ton of different priorities.

"Then why didn't you just tell me you didn't understand or see the value?" I asked. "Why didn't you just say no? Why didn't you challenge my request?"

"We knew you wouldn't like it," Jake replied. "We didn't want to frustrate you."

As we peeled the onion, I explained that this was just a first step to quarterly forecasting. By talking with each other and listening to each other's point of view, we ended up on the same page and reconnected with the other two members of my leadership team. We cleared the air, and I got a commitment that I was comfortable with. And they delivered it.

There were several positive outcomes from this breakdown. I realized that Jake and my financial controller had really strong aversions to conflict, which was really weird given what they do successfully for a living. This is when I committed to making "no" a positive so I could count on "yes." I introduced the "power of the positive no" to my team and started working to inculcate it into everything we did.

Another very powerful lightbulb moment was that when I asked them to have the team begin to start forecasting on a weekly basis, no one asked any questions. They just committed to a date and moved on. If you ask a team member to work on something and they don't ask any questions, they don't understand. Or worse, they don't agree and aren't comfortable telling you. Either way, you won't get the results you are looking for. This is when I started asking four questions to ensure I have negotiated a good commitment.

1. What are your planned next steps to tackle this assignment?

2. How do you feel about this request?

3. What is your understanding of its value to the business?

4. What do you need from me to help you succeed?

EXERCISE: CREATE MEETING AGENDAS

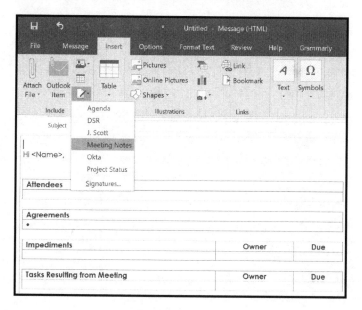

If you aren't already employing meeting agendas as a tool to prepare you to lead and allow meeting participants to show up prepared, now is the time. Start with your reoccurring meetings, and follow the instructions in the section above to develop agendas for each of them. Then commit to taking the time to develop an agenda for each meeting you schedule in the future. If you're thinking, *Why me? I would rather delegate this to someone on my team; I am too busy for this,* you are still thinking like a boss.

Remember, leaders go first; they model and then master great habits before asking their team to change. Culture is driven top-down, and leadership requires preparation. If you aren't preparing to lead, neither will your team members. You can demand it from them, but you will get mediocre results. If you start driving productive meetings that achieve outcomes your team feels good about, they will follow. In an agile environment the team leader prepares the agenda, takes the notes, and serves their team so they can focus on the heavy lifting. When your team is successful, you are successful.

If you like the idea of using Outlook signatures to create templates, you can download and import the ones we have created for agendas, meeting notes, DSRs, and project status reports here: http://info.120vc.com/outlooksignatures.

EXERCISE: PUBLISH MEETING NOTES, LOG AND TRACK COMMITMENTS

Vision:
Roadmap:

Agenda	Owner	Time Allotted
Review Meetings Rules of Engagement	Team	3 min
Review Product Score Card	Team	3 min
Weekly Standup (Sprint Review) 1. Review the Back Log and provide status on the progress of last week's commitments and their blockers.	Product Owner	8 min
Next Period Planning (Sprint Retrospective & Planning) 2. Review the Back Log, prioritize, and provide commitments for this week's planned accomplishments.	Product Owner	8 min
After Party 3. Collaborate on solutions to blockers. **Key Point:** Release team members from the meeting that aren't necessary to develop solutions to current blockers.	Product Owner	8 min

In a book titled *The 4 Disciplines of Execution*, the authors tell a story about a local football game being played shortly after hurricane Katrina blew down their scoreboard. What made the game different is that instead of the usual cheering, all you could hear was the hum of conversation in the stands. The fans couldn't concentrate on the game because they had no idea which down it was or which team was in the lead. The hum was the fans trying to find out what was happening on the field, turning to the person beside them for information because they were all lost.

Now that you are using agendas to prepare yourself to lead productive meetings, cultivating good commitments using PAVEM, and making "no" a positive so you can count on "yes," it's time to start helping your team members stay accountable to those commitments. Helping team members with accountability isn't waving your finger in someone's face when they have let you down. Leadership and accountability involve proactively ensuring you have done everything you could to set them up for success in the first place.

Don't get me wrong, your team members will have every intention of keeping their commitments, and it is important to remember you are increasing transparency and intentionality for obtaining commitments in an effort to improve performance. However, your team isn't in the habit of committing, tracking, and living this level of accountability. Like any habit, the habit of accountability is something that has to be intentionally developed.

Help them get there by publishing meetings notes that capture the agreements and task assignments that were committed to in meetings. Post the task assignments in a central repository that your team members can access (a backlog). Add an agenda item in a weekly reoccurring meeting where you pull up the backlog of tasks and have your team members provide status on their open items.

Wisdom comes with experience. Your first couple of meetings will go terribly if you expect that all of your team members will show up ready to give an update on the tasks in the backlog. A better expectation is that 2.5

percent of your team will immediately start managing all of their commitments in the backlog and will complete everything they committed to by their due dates. The rest of your team will show up and feel bad that they completely forgot about the new process and half of their commitments.

Getting to 100 percent will take about six weeks if you do the following:

1. Go over the backlog in your weekly meeting, rain or shine! If you aren't disciplined about reviewing the backlog, your team members will never develop the habit of managing their tasks in it.

2. Publicly reward adoption, even in the fourth and fifth weeks. If it took someone five weeks to finally start using the backlog, celebrate them publicly instead of making them feel like they're a laggard.

3. Privately coach the laggards until you feel that enough time has passed that they either don't have the desire or aptitude to get on board. Then help those team members find an employer with whom they can thrive.

To publish meeting notes, simply reply-all to the meeting invite, use the signature feature in Outlook to drop the meeting notes template into the body of the email, and go to work! A couple of pro tips:

- Tasks can only be assigned to a single person.
- Schedule thirty minutes after each of your meetings to get notes out and prepare for the next meeting, or you will fall behind. Notes become too old to publish by close of business the following day.
- Add the tasks to the backlog immediately following publication of the notes.

If you want detailed step-by-step instructions on planning and leading meetings, publishing notes, and tracking tasks, you can download an excerpt from our project management guidebook called "The Art of Leading Meetings" here: http://info.12ovc.com/theartofmeetings.

PART TWO

COMMUNICATION IS A VEHICLE, NOT A SCAPEGOAT

PMI's 2013 Pulse of the Profession™ report revealed that $135 million is at risk for every $1 billion spent on a project.[7] Further research on the importance of effective communications uncovers that a startling 56 percent ($75 million of that $135 million) is at risk due to ineffective communications.

The report also states that 55.7 percent of projects failed because of ineffective communication.

---

7   "The Essential Role of Communications | Project Management Institute." PMI. https://www.pmi.org/learning/thought-leadership/pulse/essential-role-communications.

In the venerable words of Miles Davis, "So what?" What can you do with this information? What is ineffective communication? I think a better question would be to ask, "Why do we communicate?" Why do project leaders communicate? Why do executives communicate? The answer is simple: they communicate to help ensure their organizations achieve the desired outcomes.

Project failure is another broad and practically useless term in that it means that a project failed to achieve one or all desired outcomes. Again, "So what?" How do you improve outcomes? Is there one solution that will improve all outcomes? Is effective communication the panacea that will solve all problems, end hunger, and achieve world peace?

I have good news: the answer is leadership. A leader's purpose is to enable the successful completion of the desired outcomes. And leadership is the skillset and ideology that, when mastered, does solve all problems—and to some degree, that includes hunger and peace.

So, if you want to improve your outcomes, stop blaming communication. It's just a vehicle, and one that is used to accomplish many things. Communication can be used to get your social needs met, to learn something, and to connect with others. It is also the vehicle we use to *lead*. If you want your team members to be more articulate, focus on improving their communication. If you want your team members to improve their ability to achieve the desired outcomes, focus on improving your leadership acumen. 'Nuff said.

CHAPTER SIX

WE COMMUNICATE TO LEAD

The modern business world treats communication as an independent skillset and uses it as an excuse for ineffective performance—a situation that causes a blame cycle and prevents leaders and their teams from focusing on real work. When executives and managers don't get the results they expected, it's common to hear that the cause was ineffective communication. When the executives finally get frustrated by the volume of unexpected results, they launch a project to improve their organization's ability to communicate.

I guess it's more emotionally approachable to blame communication than it is to acknowledge poor leadership skills.

At 120VC, we communicate for the sole purpose of leading our projects forward, as aggressively as possible, and leading our team members to achieve transformational outcomes. Whether the communication is in person or in writing, each interaction is intended to move our projects closer to completion. Any interaction that leads to confusion, or a status report that leads to questions, is a failed attempt at leadership.

We communicate to lead...period.

If you choose to label interactions that lead to confusion as "failed attempts at communication," you will focus on improving your communication skills. Unfortunately, focusing on improving your communication skills will not guarantee improved leadership skills or better outcomes.

When you fail to get the necessary results from and for your team members, don't focus on improving your communication. Focus on improving your leadership skills. As Simon Sinek says, get your "why" right. Be clear on what you really need to improve.

One of the steps to becoming a great leader is choosing to consider interactions that lead to confusion as failed attempts at leadership as opposed to failed attempts at communication. Take responsibility for what is being heard by the person you are attempting to lead. This will quickly sharpen your leadership skills and you will more consistently achieve desired outcomes.

COMMUNICATION'S ACHILLES' HEEL

The problem with focusing on improving communication as a way of improving your outcomes is that it almost always leads to more communication. More emails, voice messages, text messages, Slack messages, and meetings. This ultimately creates the need for more processes and governance over communication.

Unfortunately, this approach will create more administrative work and increased expectations for a group of people that are already struggling to achieve the expected results. When has that ever improved results?

At this point we know that leadership is about change and change is about people. We also know that leaders help their team members achieve expected results. Leaders are responsible for the outcomes. If you aren't getting the outcomes you need, blaming communication will increase the workload, but it won't guarantee better results.

On the other hand, focusing on improving your leadership skills gives you much more latitude for improving your outcomes. You aren't hamstrung by a narrow focus on improving communication. Instead of increasing workload in the name of improving communication, you could actually reduce workload to focus the team and achieve better results. You could eliminate and refine processes, educate team members, and refine software tools.

You could even eliminate communication methods! Why not abandon email for anything other than reporting and coordination? Email is a procrastination tool. We send an email and wait. We put the fate of our commitments in the hands of the responder instead of picking up the phone and calling, stopping by their office, or sending text messages.

Some years ago, I worked with DirecTV, and there was a huge push from the CIO to improve project outcomes. The majority of projects were delivered late and over budget, and IT was making promises to sales and marketing they couldn't keep.

Instead of getting a baseline of where the project managers were, from an education perspective, or a baseline of what the project managers were and were not doing, they worked from the premise that most projects failed due to ineffective communication. They created a ton of additional processes, requiring more communication, project reviews, and checkpoints where project leaders would have to get their work reviewed. They essentially increased the administrative workload; took away autonomy, mastery, and purpose; and expected better results.

Things went from bad to worse!

DirecTV had hundreds of people in their IT department and they struggled to complete projects on time and on budget. On the other hand, Trader Joe's is a national food chain with a thirty-person IT department, and they hit deadlines. What they don't manage internally is outsourced to vendors. They make it work because they have a lean, purpose-driven process with intense focus on leadership and connection between their team members; they don't do anything if it doesn't somehow benefit their team members in the stores or their customers.

The bottom line is...we communicate to *lead*. If you aren't getting the outcomes you need, focus on improving your organization's leadership skills.

MY NAME IS JASON AND I AM A RECOVERING BOSS

This is going to hurt a little, so I am just going to rip the Band-Aid off! If you aren't getting the outcomes you need, the problem is you. Accept it, stop focusing on the symptoms, and focus on improving leadership skills.

If you focus on improving your communication, you won't necessarily improve your outcomes. If you focus on improving your leadership, you'll improve your leadership and your outcomes. If you focus on improving your leadership and your team's leadership, you will supercharge your outcomes.

That said, very intelligent people will continue to stand up in front of hundreds and say, "Most projects fail because of ineffective communication," and people will eat it up. Highly paid executives will direct their teams to revamp and create layer upon layer of process to improve communication in hopes of improving project results—a clearly misguided endeavor.

It's much easier to say, "Maybe we're not getting communication right" than "We kind of suck at this leadership thing." The truth is...admitting you are possibly a shitty leader is a big win, because we are capable of improving anything we focus on improving. It's really not that hard to develop better habits if we are committed and intentional. The only obstacle is admitting we need improvement.

I am a good leader today because I admitted years ago that I was a shitty leader; I was a boss. And because I committed to becoming a great leader, now I am working on going from good to great. Like all things, I am a work in progress!

EXERCISE: START WEEKLY PERFORMANCE JOURNALING

In their *Harvard Business Review* article titled "Making Business Personal," the authors describe the deliberately developmental organization (DDO).[8] The basic premise is that the DDO structures its business practices on the assumption that people can grow. Mistakes are not vulnerabilities; rather, they are prime opportunities for personal growth. When team members grow, there is a significant and positive impact to the DDO's bottom line.

This is particularly important for the improvement of leadership in an organization. If the expectation of our executives and managers is that they *shouldn't* make any mistakes, people in those positions are less likely to acknowledge and work on their mistakes. They are more likely to spend time covering them up than acknowledging them for the sake of deliberately developing their leadership skills.

The notions that people learn the most from mistakes and that innovation requires risk-taking are not new. If asked, my CEO clients would scoff at the mere suggestion that their leadership team *shouldn't* make mistakes. In fact,

---

8   Andy Fleming, Robert Kegan, Lisa Lahey, and Matthew Miller. "Making Business Personal." Harvard Business Review. November 13, 2015. https://hbr.org/2014/04/making-business-personal.

my clients frequently tell me that they want innovators and entrepreneurs on their teams.

Then, the first thing their organization does when a problem occurs is find someone to blame.

The most important enabler of leadership development is an organizational culture that "in action" not only embraces mistakes, but is a culture that creates frequent, reoccurring, and public forums that are safe to explore those mistakes. The first step to creating this type of forum is to understand the Kolb experiential learning model, otherwise known as the adult learning model.[9]

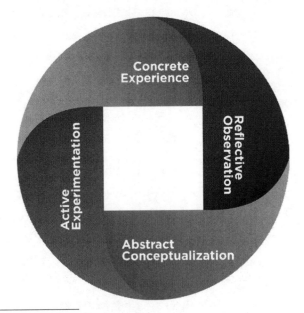

9 David A. Kolb, *Experiential Learning: Experience as the Source of Learning and Development.* Upper Saddle River, NJ: Pearson Education, 2015.

Kolb found that for an adult to learn or grow, we need to stop and intentionally reflect on what we learned in a training session or from the outcome of our own actions, taking time to reflect on the recent past for the sake of improvement and then conceptualize how we can apply what we learned or can improve upon our results. Once you have an idea of what improvement looks like, decide on a future approach and seek opportunities to experiment with that approach.

A simple and low-cost way to begin deliberately developing your leadership skills is to begin keeping a weekly leadership performance journal (pJournal). The pJournal is a simple tool developed by the Stagen Leadership Academy that employs the adult learning model and the cultural components necessary to maximize the opportunities associated with mistakes.

The pJournal format:

1. Mental replay of a "concrete experience"
   - The situation: describe what happened:
   - Results: describe the results, consequences, implications:

2. Reflection: "reflective observation"
   - My thoughts: describe what I was thinking:
   - My behavior: describe what I did and said:

- My inner state: describe what I was feeling:

3. Self-authoring: "abstract conceptualization"
   - Key insights: describe your triggers, habits, patterns:
   - Desired outcome: describe what I really want:
   - Action: describe what my next step is or what you will do next time:

CRITERIA FOR A GOOD PJOURNAL

1. Identify a leadership mistake you made: a situation that you wish you had handled better with other people in the room, on a call, or via email. Ultimately, the premise of the exercise is to identify a situation that you *did not* influence and where you failed to attain the result you were hoping for from other people.

2. Remember that you are the only thing in this world you have complete control over. Your insights in the journal and actions/next steps should be yours. Do not list next steps that involve other people's actions.

3. The main outcome of this exercise is to take the time to work through the situation, evaluate your actions/results, and *commit* to how you will handle the next similar situation. When you are done with

the exercise each week, you will have a roadmap to experiment for the purpose of refining your ability to influence people and improve your leadership skills.

UNDERSTANDING SITUATIONAL LEADERSHIP

Today's business world consists of various forms of communication that lend themselves to particular outcomes. Email, phone, text, meetings, and in-person dialogue all play a role, and it is important to adjust your communication methods to the task and team at hand, rather than vice versa.

CHOOSING THE BEST VEHICLE

My talent acquisition team, which includes two recruiters and a pair of account executives, has weekly video conference calls to discuss the recruiting pipeline and process improvements. The account executives are responsible for client accounts, through which clients make requests for services. If we don't have internal team members to fulfill those services, my recruiters set out to hire talent.

On one particular occasion, we were talking about the relationship between our average number of openings and the average number of them we were able to hire and fulfill. At the time, our ability to hire and fulfill opportunities was terribly low. We had a ton of demand, but we struggled to find qualified candidates to put to work, and we were losing deals. The team call included a lot of brainstorming on process improvements, and something about Karen—my lead recruiter—caught my eye. She wasn't saying much, and she sat slumped in her chair. All of her answers were fine and she participated in the conversation, but her body language made it clear there was something she wasn't happy about.

All of my team members publish a daily status report. It consists of three *gratitudes*, or things the person is grateful for, two or three accomplishments, and a plan for two or three things they plan to accomplish the next day. We start with gratitudes because consulting is difficult, and gratitudes help us focus on the positive. The accomplishments are next, and the act of documenting them causes your brain to release dopamine. Planning for the next day is just good practice and allows you to visualize things you need to get done. The team publishes their daily reports to our collaboration tool, as this practice allows for autonomy and for others to lean in and help when needed.

On this particular day, I looked at Karen's daily status report, and one of her gratitudes read "Monday is over." I thought, "Well, that can't be good," because that's certainly not a gratitude; it sounded more like a complaint. I responded immediately and asked what was going on and if I could help. She wrote back that somewhere in the meeting she'd heard me say "recruiting is broken." I assure you I didn't say that; I'm much more intentional about how I message. She had heard the numbers needed to improve but internalized it as "recruiting is broken."

We didn't have the luxury of video conference, as I was away on business, but I felt I needed to call her right away because operating under the assumption that the CEO thinks she's broken is not a healthy place for my recruiter to be. I got her on the phone and asked her to tell me more. I listened and asked clarifying questions. I told her my intention wasn't to communicate that recruiting was broken, only that that we needed to improve the numbers. I explained the entire team needed to do better, not just recruiting.

After the conversation, she thanked me for calling and said she felt better. It was obvious in the days that followed that her mood was no longer dark. She was engaged and happy, and brought positive energy. The moral of the story is that I would not have realized she had been negatively impacted had I not been able to see her body language. There's no way I could have connected with her and addressed her concerns via text or email, as she needed to hear in my voice that I cared and wasn't just addressing business. I needed to be able to listen to her and ask questions, and she needed to hear the sincerity of my concern for her well-being—ultimately, that's what turned it around.

Don't get me wrong: not everything has to be done over the phone or in person. As a leader, you can identify situations where leadership is required. If there's a presentation that needs to be picked up from the printer and I know a team member is driving by on the way to the office, I can text the request and ask them to pick it up. It's simple, and there's a high degree of likelihood I'll get the outcome I am looking for. The more emotionally charged a situation, the greater the need for an in-person meeting, or at least a video conference call.

COMMUNICATING TO LEAD

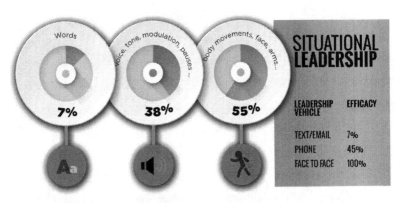

As we discussed in Chapter 1, the Mehrabian model shows us that we only get 7 percent of someone's feeling through their words, 38 percent through voice modulation, and 55 percent through body movement.

It's not unusual for people's words to communicate the

opposite of what they really mean. In terms of leadership effectiveness, I can only be 7 percent effective with text or email. If I add words to voice tone modulation, I get 45 percent, a combination of those two. If I add words and voice tone modulation to my body movements, I add 55 percent more clarity and the ability to be 100 percent effective with all of my listening and empathy skills. Empathy, concern, and genuine curiosity are communicated much more clearly through our body language than our words. Being able to see a team member also allows me to listen with more than just my ears; I can listen with my eyes because I'll get more from what I *see* they're communicating than from what they say.

LEADERSHIP REQUIRES FACE-TO-FACE TIME

You aren't leading your team if you don't spend time with them. This is a *big deal*. Many executives and managers are "super busy," their door is always closed, and they have a tendency to cancel or "push" one-to-one meetings because "the team's fine." When they do need to interact with their team, they choose the most efficient way, that is, the one that takes the least amount of their time. In my experience, you can be efficient with things, not with people. With people, taking the long way tends to get you to your destination faster.

Let's say I ask somebody to create a proposal for a client.

We discuss the proposal, and they ask me questions. Then they put it together and email it to me. I open the document and realize it's not what I wanted; I think it could be organized better, and I have a number of criticisms. I have a couple of choices:

1. I can fix it myself, but that's not leadership. Ultimately, it also communicates to the team member that I don't believe they are capable, and I rob them of the opportunity to learn or grow from the exercise.

2. I can redline it back and have them make the changes. This is efficient in terms of time, but will they learn anything? How are they going to feel about the fact that I redlined all the changes? Did I really give critical feedback? Remember, the reason we give critical feedback is so our team members can grow and improve, so the next time they can get closer to the target. It's an investment in your team member.

3. I can swing by their office and spend time face-to-face going over it. This is the ideal situation, because receiving critical feedback is always difficult. Any conversation where somebody learns their work—what they did, what they built, what they delivered—didn't hit the mark is going to be a hard conversation. If I do it in person, they can see that I am coming from a caring place. Think about that and be empathetic.

Ask their permission to provide critical feedback; let them know you've found areas for improvement in the proposal and would like to go over it in person. Nine times out of ten, they will agree. Make sure to let them know that it's perfectly fine if now is not the best time and schedule a future time.

EXERCISE: GIVE CRITICAL FEEDBACK

Leadership will frequently require giving critical feedback in the form of coaching, and this exercise will help you get the results you are hoping for from the coaching sessions. Pick a team member that you feel could improve in some way. Not your problem child; it's better to practice on a high performer, someone that generally gets positive feedback and because of their performance is generally overlooked from a coaching perspective.

The first step is to plan the conversation. Take a few minutes to write down the situation, the individual's current approach, and the impact to the business. Do not make it personal or about the team member's character; instead, keep the feedback focused on specific actions and impact to the business. It is critical to be very specific about what you feel they need to do differently or improve. Give specific examples of what you would like to see happen differently and alternatives that they could employ.

Then it's important to ask them how they feel about the feedback, what they are taking away, and how they might approach the situation next. Then listen actively.

"Listen with a genuine desire to relate to others with dignity and curiosity."

—FRED KOFMAN

They will undoubtedly want to explain why they did it the way they did. You will undoubtedly have to fight the urge to have them focus on the way forward instead of their past actions. It is important for you to listen and let them process the feedback in their own way. If they start explaining why they did it the way they did, make a charitable assumption and don't jump to the conclusion that they are justifying their actions and pushing back on your coaching.

Listen, ask questions to understand, and restate your understanding. Then if they don't move forward and process your coaching, you can move them forward and they will let you. Because, through active listening, they know you understand their past actions and still believe firmly in your coaching.

Once you're prepared, reach out to the individual and let them know that you have some coaching that will help the two of you get better aligned, and ask their permission to connect.

The steps to effectively giving critical feedback are:

1. Take time to prepare by writing down the situation, their specific actions, and the impact to the business. Be as specific as you can, and do not conflate their actions with their character. Then write down specific examples of the alternative approach or outcomes you would like to see.

2. Meet with them face-to-face if physically possible. A video conference is okay, and phone is worst-case scenario only.

3. Let them know you would like to offer some coaching and ask if now is a good time. This gives them space to mentally prepare, and having a choice helps with the potential fight-or-flight response sometimes associated with critical feedback.

4. Describe the situation, their observable approach, the impact on the business as you see it, and the alternatives you are hoping for. Be specific.

5. Ask them how they feel about the feedback, what they are hearing, and what their takeaways are.

6. Actively listen until what you hear is predictive of the future results you are trying to achieve.

Two things to remember when you are finished with the conversation:

First, if the approach to providing constructive feedback I have outlined is different than the way you have approached coaching in the past, it won't feel natural and it might not go smoothly. Despite that, keep practicing and you will get more comfortable and achieve better results over time.

Second, leaders give critical feedback and provide coaching because we believe there is a gap between what our business needs to succeed and the results we are getting from specific team members. When this gap occurs, it is our job to fill the vacuum as quickly as possible or our business will stall and the other team members will suffer. We don't give critical feedback because we think it's fun!

If, after following these steps over the course of several feedback sessions, you have a team member that continues to refuse the feedback and adjust, it's not you, it's them. And you have done everything you are responsible for as a leader by attempting to provide them with the feedback that they need to thrive in the most productive way. If this happens, it is time to help the team member move on to an organization where they can thrive, and fill the vacuum with someone you believe will be wildly successful in the role.

In any event, I would love it if you sent me a note on LinkedIn to share how this approach to providing critical feedback is working for you!

CHAPTER SEVEN

TAKE RESPONSIBILITY FOR WHAT'S HEARD

To start this section, I'd like to tell you a story about an executive that was a dictator who took no responsibility for his team's negative outcomes.

In years past, I worked with a media powerhouse with worldwide presence, led in part by a senior vice president known for tearing people apart. Hundreds of people across the United States worked for him. On one hand, he significantly improved the global IT department's ability to deliver on client needs; on the other hand, if he didn't like something, he yelled in public, openly criticized people, and verbally beat them down. When something didn't go according to plan, the first thing he would ask is, "Who fucked it up?"

My job as a consulting project leader was to work with members of this team to move large projects forward as aggressively as possible without leaving any time or money on the table. My first challenge was getting team members to trust me. I reported to the volatile SVP, and the team didn't want to tell me anything that might get back to him and unleash a rant or potentially get them fired. Fear was viscerally evident in the organization, and it took months to convince them to get comfortable enough to work with me and trust me. Even then, they hesitated. I sat in on meetings with his direct reports and watched as they spent hours concocting stories that allowed them to move forward without tipping off the boss that things weren't always under control.

The environment was tense. The team refused to tell him things for fear of his reaction. Inevitably, he regularly received inaccurate information, and he made decisions based on this information, which created a ripple effect of problems. The team created subterfuge, he made strategic decisions, and people executed on bad information—a dynamic that, of course, transformed into a ton of extra work, terrible working conditions, an inability to share and learn from mistakes, and a complete lack of innovation.

Sadly, this was considered a highly productive department—albeit three times the size of any others in the company—and the SVP got all of the credit for increasing service levels and response times, in spite of all the work involved. At the time, I thought if we could only focus on getting the work done, the team could get 60 percent of their time back, deliver their projects 60 percent faster, and save a ton of money. They were burning money, and nobody was going to risk sharing this with the company's CEO.

To me, this particular individual represents an executive and managerial camp that feels they are not responsible for their team's outcomes unless the results are positive, and then they take the credit. They make demands, provide zero support, and make it clear that your job is constantly on the line. It makes me sick to admit that this approach gets results, but it does, though the costs are incredibly high. In this case, morale was terrible, turnover was extremely common, and the cost of running the department was three times that of any of the other departments in IT.

This executive was the epitome of a dictator, and we all know what the first three letters in that word spell. A leader takes responsibility for both good and bad outcomes. A great leader will go as far as taking responsibility for what their team members *hear* when they are making a commitment.

If you just scoffed at the impossibility of my last statement, don't stop reading, because I guarantee you will change your mind. I am about to give your confirmation bias a run for its money.

BUYER BEWARE

What made the situation in this particular company hysterical, in a not-so-funny way, was that they tried to address their organizational dysfunction by asking their vendors to find them new team members that had previous experience working at this company. They assumed that if someone had been successful there in the past, they would be able to take it. What we found was that most people that had worked there in the past would rather die and go to hell than return, and the ones that agreed to return weren't welcome back. My advice: beware the organization that feels their needs are so specific that the only people that can thrive there are their past employees!

TAKE RESPONSIBILITY FOR THE BAD OUTCOMES

The premise of taking responsibility for what is heard is that, as a leader, I am responsible for the outcome. People want to do a good job and succeed; that's how we are wired. Yes, there are lazy people in the world, but they rarely get hired into startups or high-performing corporations. First, most lazy people aren't applying for those jobs; there are plenty of jobs where you can stand around all day and do almost nothing. Second, those jobs are so competitive that it's almost impossible for a lazy person to get hired, and when they do, they don't last long.

Don't get me wrong, I'm not knocking lazy...Sometimes I envy the lazy. My point is that most people don't intentionally deliver suboptimal work; they're more likely to do nothing at all than just be average. So, when you think you get alignment on a commitment with a team member, they go work really hard, and then they deliver something other than what you expected...Who failed here?

A boss would say, "It's on them," "They should have asked more questions," "Maybe they aren't the right person for the job," or, "It's their responsibility to figure it out, and if they can't, they were a bad hire."

A leader would pause and take the opportunity to assess where the commitment got off track. They would reflect on what they could have done to ensure their team member truly had clarity, capability, and the availability to complete the task they committed to. Because in that moment—the moment the team member realizes the hours they spent working to complete their commitment resulted in something you didn't want—they feel pretty shitty.

In that moment, a leader picks them up, creates velocity toward a better outcome, and makes it a learning experience for everyone.

If you are still not convinced, I have one more concept

for you. Responsibility isn't just about signing up to be accountable when the outcome is clear or guaranteed. Ultimately, I am committed to raising my seven-year-old son and my five-year-old daughter to be productive, happy human beings. I don't know about you, but I think happy is a big commitment. I have a better chance of succeeding if I commit to ensuring my kids grow up to be astronauts rather than happy and productive. Still, I am 100 percent accountable to my commitment. I work on it every day. I have zero guarantee of success. Still, for me, that doesn't alleviate my responsibility.

Taking responsibility for something is a choice, just like being a leader is a choice. You can be a boss and get results. Leadership is about taking responsibility for what's heard. It's stepping up and saying, "You're my team. I know we're going to make mistakes. When we make mistakes, we'll focus and solve them together, and I'm going to improve my leadership skills through that exercise. We'll learn from those lessons and, ultimately, we'll succeed and fail together. That's what a team does."

Now I am going to level the playing field by explaining how you can hedge your bets and take responsibility for what's heard by ensuring you know what was heard. You didn't think I was going to leave you hanging after that kid speech did you?

LAG MEASURES AND LEAD MEASURES

People are generally familiar with lag measures. A lag measure is the traditional approach to measuring progress. Traditionally, a company sets a financial goal, the team puts in some effort, and then they look at the financial report at the end of each week to determine where they are against plan. If they are behind, all they can do is work harder, because they can't influence the past. That time is lost. There is essentially a lag between the time they put in the effort and the time they find out if they are on target or not.

Another example of a lag measure is when you collaborate with a team member to define a necessary outcome. You ask them if they are clear on the "what" by "when" and they say yes. They spend a week working hard on what they believe they agreed to, but when they deliver the result, it isn't what you thought you agreed to or what you actually need.

Failure is a lag measure.

Lead measures, on the other hand, are measures that are predictive of the intended outcome. To develop lead measures for a financial goal, you would work with your team to identify the activities necessary to accomplish that goal. In consulting sales, qualified proposals are definitely a lead measure toward a financial goal. If you don't have any proposals out, you don't have any deals in the pipeline. This is a bad place to be if you are trying to hit a financial goal. So, if your team agrees that proposals are the best lead measure, then you have to determine how many qualified proposals the team needs to send out each week. Let's assume the team agreed on a target of thirty proposals per week, and on the first week only twenty-five have been sent out by Thursday; it's time to rally the team and hit the phones. On the other hand, if thirty-two proposals have been sent out by Thursday, maybe everyone gets to work a half day Friday.

You would still use the lag measure of reviewing the financial results at the end of the week, but its purpose is to refine your lead measure. If you hit thirty each week for three weeks, but you are behind on your financial goal overall, you need to increase your lead measure target. If you are at thirty and far exceeding your financial goal, you might want to decrease the lead measure target if your team is killing themselves to get thirty proposals out.

Another lead measure example is to measure your food intake and exercise if you want to lose weight. It's not unusual for people to set a weight loss goal only to be disappointed at the end of the week when they are behind their goal at weigh-in. If you have been sedentary and eating whatever you want, it wouldn't be crazy to assume you would lose weight if you committed to walking three miles, five days a week and limiting your food intake to two thousand calories per day. Then, instead of waiting until the end of the week to get on the scale, measure the number of days you put in three miles and kept it under two thousand calories. If you didn't stick to your lead measure target, you aren't going to hit your lag measure goal.

LISTENING IS A LEAD MEASURE

The next time you collaborate with a team member to define a necessary outcome, don't ask if they are clear on the "what" by "when." Ask them to run you through their understanding of the commitment and what their next steps will be. What they describe is predictive of the results you are going to get. If their explanation does not sound like the outcome you need, it's not semantics; it's a clear indicator that you were not on the same page. Now, instead of waiting days to learn they were unclear, you can clarify in the moment. Continue working to get aligned until what they describe and their chosen next steps sound like they will accomplish the outcome you are expecting.

This isn't micromanagement. Your team member is determining the next steps and describing what they think they have just committed to. By doing this, you are saving the time that would be lost if they weren't truly clear. You are also preventing them from the negative emotions associated with working hard only to deliver something that doesn't hit the mark.

You are taking responsibility for what was heard.

The next time you ask someone if they are clear on something and they say yes, remember all of the times that wasn't true and laugh at yourself. Then ask them to clarify their understanding and next steps.

EXERCISE: START LEADING WITH LEAD MEASURES

The next time you lead a meeting, ask anyone that commits to a "what" by "when" to run you through their understanding of their commitment and what their steps to accomplish it will be. My go-to questions are:

1. Okay, now run me through what you believe you just committed to do and the planned next steps.

2. What are you hearing? How will completing this benefit the business?

3. How do you feel about this assignment?

4. Now that we are clear on the "what" by "when," what do you need from me?

BABY STEPS ARE GOLD

Kmart is a longtime national brand that was once as popular in American culture as baseball and apple pie. In 2000, they launched a $1.4 billion IT modernization project to refresh their technology infrastructure to regain competitiveness with Walmart and Target. What they ended up with was so highly customized that maintenance alone was cost-prohibitive and required a $600 million supply chain software upgrade. The project completely derailed in 2002 and contributed to Kmart's decision to merge with Sears—another tale of woe.

Kmart's story is important because there was a lack of common sense at play. When you look at an organization that has lost its competitive advantage, common sense dictates its culture is no longer competitive. Wholesale change from an IT infrastructure perspective affects the way everyone in the organization does their job, and the likelihood of them being ready for a change of this magnitude is zero.

Kmart made the big mistake of assuming they were capable of making a company-wide change to regain market share. They thought the entire employee base would get behind it because they wanted to win. That, of course, didn't happen, because they didn't have a culture of people prepared to deal with such a dramatic change.

A more effective approach would have been to break

up the tech refresh into bite-size projects prioritized by business value, with the highest-value initiatives first, then hand-select a dedicated project team for a single initiative, and begin moving the needle. As that project team delivers business value, publicly applaud them and the results their project is driving within the competitive landscape. Celebrating publicly will drive adoption of the new business model and foster a desire for more change.

When the first project is complete, celebrate big and give that team another project. And then hand-select a second team, dedicate them, and run two projects in parallel. With the completion of each project, you increase your change readiness and ability to tackle more change. Remember, baby steps are gold.

When you're losing, it's easy to feel desperate and like you need to make massive investments quickly. Don't! You will probably burn time and money and destroy relationships you need for success. Remember that you didn't end up in this situation overnight, and you won't get out of it overnight either. That said, you do need to change quickly, just not in one giant leap. Create a two-year vision *with* your team. Identify all of the changes that need to be made to become competitive again, including the need to fall in love with the market leader in your space. Then break up the plan into little projects and start running!

EXERCISE: BEGIN CONDUCTING RECURRING WEEKLY PROJECT TEAM MEETINGS

Identify a struggling project, schedule a recurring weekly meeting to focus on it, and make it sacred. Not every individual you need to drive the project forward as aggressively or efficiently as possible is going to be available next week or the week after, but if you leave it in the same spot, over time, their schedules will clear up and they will show up.

Vision:
Roadmap:

Agenda	Owner	Time Allotted
Review Meetings Rules of Engagement	Team	3 min
Review Product Score Card	Team	3 min
Weekly Standup (Sprint Review) 1. Review the Back Log and provide status on the progress of last week's commitments and their blockers.	Product Owner	8 min
Next Period Planning (Sprint Retrospective & Planning) 2. Review the Back Log, prioritize, and provide commitments for this week's planned accomplishments.	Product Owner	8 min
After Party 3. Collaborate on solutions to blockers. **Key Point:** Release team members from the meeting that aren't necessary to develop solutions to current blockers.	Product Owner	8 min

This weekly meeting will allow you to incorporate several of the principles we have discussed in the book so far—making change a habit, identifying stories, leadership requires preparation, PAVEM, meeting notes, and the backlog—and this meeting will become your first cadence of accountability, your first baby step.

UNCOVERING THE ROOTS OF RESISTANCE

In the past, I had trouble empathizing with people's resistance to their own commitments. I would watch team members set goals for themselves, only to make every excuse to avoid the work they'd committed to. They seemed to work against themselves, and all it did was frustrate me! I would say to them, "Just say no!" At least then I could assign the work to someone else and ensure predictable outcomes.

At other times, I found myself spending hours helping a team member prioritize their workload so they could find the time to keep their commitments and achieve their goals. And still they would fail to get the job done. I was left to conclude they were just resistant and unreliable.

An easy analogy is that friend of yours that commits to going to the gym before work and then struggles daily to get out of bed. My advice was always "Just get up! What's the problem? You made a commitment; just do it!"

Then, a couple of years ago, my CEO coach, Mark Murphy, helped me understand resistance. He sent me a podcast by Matthew Kelly, founder and CEO of Dynamic Catholic. The podcast is from the *Best Lent Ever* series, titled "Day 1: Resistance." Now, I am not a religious person, but the podcast opened my eyes and helped me develop the tools to actually help team members work through their cognitive dissonance.

In the podcast, Kelly describes resistance as a physical, visceral reaction to a situation or even a thought. He starts out by asking if you have ever hit the snooze button. I'm thinking, *Who hasn't?* Then he says, "No big deal right? But it is a big deal. Resistance just kicked your butt."

I don't know why, but I was suddenly projected back to the last time I hit the snooze button. I reflected on how I was feeling and remembered the weight I felt on my body in the moment. I felt heavy, like the last thing in the world I wanted to do was get up.

Then I remembered standing on the back of my boat debating with friends if we should go scuba diving. All of that gear is so heavy and such a pain in the ass to get out, put on, clean up, and put away. I reminded myself that even though it's a lot of work, I always have a great time. So we went. And finally, I was struck by something that had just happened.

I live in the Pacific Northwest, and when the sun comes out in the winter, everybody gets outside. I was working at home in my flip-flops and lunch rolled around. I looked outside and considered taking my motorcycle for a ride to get food. Then I thought about getting the helmet out, getting the jacket on, and putting the gloves on, and realized I needed to change my shoes. So, I grabbed my truck keys and went to lunch. This was my snooze-button moment! It would have taken me no time to get out the gear and change my shoes. The equipment isn't heavy; it doesn't require sailing anywhere. Resistance kicked my butt over a tiny insignificant thing: changing my shoes!

In that moment, I realized that my perspective on resistance was wrong. I wasn't impervious to it and I wasn't as self-aware as I would like to be. I always thought that my team members were just choosing to be unaccountable, and I expected them to make better decisions. So I pushed, I insisted, I micromanaged, but I didn't help them transcend their resistance.

With newfound empathy for resistance—the feeling, the pressure, the cognitive dissonance—I stopped pushing and started asking questions. It's amazing what you can learn when you empathetically point out that someone's words are not congruent to their actions, ask them why, and then actively listen to their response. Through the course of an active listening exercise, I have had grown men and women realize they were avoiding because of fear or even shame. They were able to unpack the story they had developed in their heads surrounding these activities and realize the stories weren't congruent with their reality. They could then admit to themselves how easy it was to justify their inability to complete those activities and claim they were too busy.

Once they realize their unconscious resistance, it becomes really easy for them to make a choice. They can choose to recommit and set different goals or realize they are in a position at a company that isn't right for them. Either way, uncovering the roots of their resistance gives them clarity and choice. They could comfortably say, "No, I don't think I really want to sign up for that," or choose with clarity to tackle their original goals.

Ultimately, empathizing and listening as a way to help them work through their lack of congruence leads to a collaborative decision on the way forward and, ultimately, much more reliable commitments.

EXERCISE: DEFINE YOUR SNOOZE-BUTTON MOMENT

Fact: You encounter resistance every day. In the workplace, at home, and with your friends. As a leader, it's your job to help your team members unpack their resistance to find a way forward. In doing so, you are doing everything you can to help them reach for *their* potential. You can give them opportunity, but they ultimately need to find success.

To become adept at this, I invite you to define your

snooze-button moment. If you're frustrated with some-one's resistance or lack of accountability, stop and take five minutes to reflect on and get deeply connected with *your* snooze-button moment. Remember, you're a human being, too. You're not a machine and neither are they. Your frustration is because you expect them to simply "get it done" and function through their cognitive dissonance. The resistance can be anywhere from mild to physically daunting. Go explore it with them; help them unlock it. Help them feel safe, and get them to talk about it.

The entire purpose of identifying your snooze-button moment is to stay grounded when you're pissed off that someone won't get on board. It's easy to forget in the moment. We are drivers, but remember, leaders play for their team members. That frustration you feel is tied to you wanting what you want when you want it. It's not about helping them be the best they can be.

Last, if the time comes, letting unproductive team members go is hard, and it's important to feel like you did everything you could to help them succeed. Working with them to unpack their resistance will enable you to handle that situation with the grace and dignity every human being deserves. It also sets them up to take this opportunity to find a job in a company where they can thrive.

PART THREE

A CULTURE OF ACCOUNTABILITY

If you surveyed all of the workers in the US and asked them if they would prefer to work for a leader or a manager, I suspect most would say a leader. Why? Because nobody wants to be managed! We know that once you pay someone enough to eliminate their financial concerns, they are motivated by autonomy, mastery, and purpose.

Since managers (like bosses) feel it's in their best interest to tell their team members what to do, autonomy seems unlikely under management.

Here's the rub: if our team members don't employ a high degree of personal accountability, the best leaders are forced to manage. Much like the feedback receiver is in 100 percent control over whether they receive feedback constructively or negatively, regardless of how skillfully the coaching was delivered, our team members are 100 percent in control over whether they receive leadership or management.

Leadership only works if our team members own their responsibilities. We need our team members to consider their roles and ideate. Identify the way forward and develop solutions for all situations. Then when they are vetting solutions or communicating their approach to a shared goal, their leader gets to play coach, collaborator, and coconspirator.

If, on the other hand, our team members are constantly showing up with updates on progress with no solutions for the way forward, their leader will have no choice but to tell them what to do—because the show must go on!

CHAPTER EIGHT

ACCOUNTABILITY IS GENEROUS AND KIND

If you master every recommendation I have made so far but fail to create a culture of accountability, you will have a really nice team that gets nothing done. The cornerstones of a high-performing team are trust and accountability.

And I don't know a single person that gets excited when the topic of accountability comes up. Most of us see it as a chore, a burden, or a necessary evil. This is because most of us start out in life with a negative perception of accountability. When we are toddlers, our parents set boundaries to keep us alive, and as we grow, they work to help us become healthy members of society.

However, as toddlers, we can't possibly see those boundaries as anything other than a punishment. We want to do something, and they won't let us! So, we keep pushing, and the third time I try to put my hand on the hot stove, my dad smacks it in an attempt to deter any further exploration.

As we get older, we try to explain why they are making a shortsighted decision to prevent us from getting our needs met. If we could only get them to see how badly we want to eat that entire box of cookies, surely they would concede to our logic. But for some reason they just don't listen. So we sneak the cookies into our room at bedtime, eat the entire box, wake up, vomit all over the bed, and then get grounded for a week.

Boundaries suck and end up being interpreted as punishments. As we get older, we get introduced to the words "responsibility" and "accountability" by our parents, and they seem to be the teenage versions of boundaries and punishment.

Ultimately, this shapes our perception of accountability as something we would rather avoid, or something that is easiest to do when we are angry. As a leader, accountability is simply acknowledging that something has stalled so we can find a way forward.

Bosses "hold people accountable." The phrase itself

sounds like they are physically accosting someone. When they don't get the results they expect, they become frustrated because of the negative impact this situation will have on their success. So they get busy "holding people accountable" and looking for someone to blame. It can be brutal.

Because of our childhood experience with accountability and the way that bosses model accountability, it remains people's least favorite leadership responsibility.

The problem with the story we tell ourselves about accountability is that we know it's not true. If someone knew you were about to make a mistake or drop the ball on a commitment, you would want them to tell you. If someone more experienced than you could help you improve and be more successful by offering constructive criticism, you would want them to. If your manager thought you were underperforming and let you go without ever telling you, you would be shocked! You would feel like they didn't care enough about you as a human being to give you the feedback you needed to be successful.

So, when a leader is willing to have an uncomfortable conversation to help a team member be more successful, it is both generous and kind. When they are willing to step outside of their comfort zone and risk being disliked because they've chosen to play for their team members, it is a gift.

EXERCISE: LAST-STRAW MOMENTS

In this exercise, make a list of ten instances when you gave critical feedback. The first two or three will come easy, but it will get progressively more difficult to think of others. Keep going until you can't anymore or until you hit ten. For each event, record the following:

- Did you wait to provide the critical feedback until you became frustrated or the problem got too big? Why?
- Were there opportunities to address the problems earlier?
- If you had given the feedback at the first opportunity and followed the instructions in Chapter 7 for giving critical feedback, would the outcome have been different?

After answering the above questions for each instance, evaluate where you are on the feedback spectrum. Do you give regular feedback to the point where your team members see coaching as part of the job? Do you see accountability/giving critical feedback as a chore or as generous and kind? Where can you improve?

Then commit to a feedback improvement goal and block

thirty minutes on your calendar each week to reflect on the feedback you gave over the past week. During the thirty-minute time block, evaluate the feedback you gave during the past week against your goal and think about how you could make adjustments to get better results. Then spend the next week putting those adjustments to the test.

IT STARTS WITH YOU

The first stop on the way to a high-accountability culture is you. If you aren't comfortable offering constant, rich feedback in the form of coaching, it will be difficult for someone to receive it as comfortable when you provide it. So, instead of asking you to practice getting comfortable giving critical feedback to your team members, I am going to start by asking you to begin critically evaluating yourself.

Leaders need to hold themselves to the same high standards of performance they expect from their team members. We expect our team members to take time to evaluate themselves and set improvement goals. We get frustrated with them when it feels like we have to constantly coach them because they aren't self-evaluating and improving.

The big question: when was the last time you took thirty

minutes to reflect, evaluate your performance, and set improvement goals? If you don't do this intentionally, you aren't improving, at least not quickly. At the end of Chapter 6, we had a performance journaling exercise. If you did this, you are once again prepared to lead, to be the first to go into the unknown, and to model the behavior you want from your team.

I began using the performance journal to create velocity for my improvement as a leader. Once I felt comfortable with the journals and my ability to be honest with myself, I began publishing them to my team. Coaching is done in private but taking individual responsibility for the team's outcomes is best done in public.

If you want each of your team members to start taking responsibility for their contribution to the team's outcomes, show them how. Publicly taking responsibility for your contribution to the team's outcomes doesn't abdicate them of their responsibility. It instead makes it safe to do the same and shines a spotlight on those that don't or won't take responsibility.

I own every one of my improvement goals publicly. My journals create a healthy discipline personally and a healthy dialogue within my team. I take time to go over the game film and admit failure. If I fuck up, I write it on the wall, figure out how I would like to handle the situation in the future, commit to those actions, and share it with my team.

Remember, commitments are best when they are public, active, voluntary, explicit, and mission-focused. If we benefit from getting public commitments for improvement from our team, we benefit by making public commitments.

Executives are traditionally taught to "never let them see you sweat," but I've learned it's the exact opposite. You empower people and foster trust through vulnerability, and trust creates velocity. I cannot think of a more powerful way to encourage your team to feel comfortable with self-evaluation. This practice creates a culture of vulnerability in which people are capable of owning their improvement because that behavior is modeled from the top.

Full disclosure: the first time I shared a performance journal with my team, it was impulsive. I felt like it was the right thing to do; I believed it was the best next step to help them feel comfortable owning their contribution to our business challenges, but I was nervous. I sat there, hovering over the send button for two minutes, trying to figure out how this could go wrong. I finally said "fuck it" and hit send.

At this point, I've lost count of the number of times people have said, "I can't believe you just shared that." And I wouldn't have it any other way. In a very positive way, this vulnerability moves my team emotionally and builds a bond. They see authenticity, my thoughts, my feelings, and the ideas that resonate with me.

When someone does something we think is kind, generous, or *vulnerable*, we see it as a gift and want to reciprocate. In business, this allows us as a team to improve and commit publicly, to improve without the leader actually addressing a need or pointing a finger at anyone.

A CULTURE OF ACCOUNTABILITY REQUIRES THE TEAM TO MASTER THREE DISCIPLINES:

1. Public self-evaluation and improvement

2. Peer accountability in the form of feedback and coaching

3. A leader that has mastered the ability to deliver critical feedback productively

Earlier in the book, I talked about how Douglas Stone teaches that the receiver is 100 percent in control of whether they take feedback and coaching as constructive or dismiss it as BS. I find that people are more willing to accept feedback from people they know are self-evaluating and improving. If they know you aren't above giving yourself feedback and accepting critical feedback from others, they are more willing to perceive you as a trustworthy source of feedback and coaching.

CAPITALIZE ON AWARENESS

Over time, performance journaling helped me identify trends in situations that triggered me. For example, I don't love talking about finances. It doesn't matter if the numbers are positive or negative; I get emotionally heightened. This became obvious to me after I saw the number of performance journals that were generated after our weekly finance meeting.

This realization and sharing my performance journal helped me in two ways: I got intentional about preparing myself to be calm before our finance meetings, and my team was enabled to help me if I slipped. When I got triggered, they were ready to help me take a break and reset. One time in particular, I started getting frustrated about something and one of my team members said, "J, dude...Whoosah!" and we all started laughing!

That is the work of a high-functioning team. I help them stay accountable, and they help me! There is no boss. Just a high-functioning, highly accountable team where each individual is willing and safe to point out when we aren't being accountable and lift us up.

DON'T BE TOO BUSY TO GROW

In Chapter 3, I talked about being intentional about planning the coming week and blocking time on my calendar to work on my priorities. To make my leadership development a priority, I have a weekly reoccurring meeting on my calendar for Fridays at 9:00 a.m. If I didn't block time to stop and reflect on my performance in the form of a performance journal each week, I would just continue to act out of habit.

If you haven't already, I invite you to be intentional about your development as a leader by blocking time each week to complete a performance journal. In order for us to learn, we first need to have concrete experience, to reflect on that experience, and to actively experiment. If we don't ever stop (and we don't most of the time), we are simply acting out our existing habits. In that space between action and reaction, the discipline to cultivate choice won't happen if we don't intentionally work on it. We don't learn anything on the meeting merry-go-round, and busy managers aren't good leaders.

ACCOUNTABILITY PRACTICES IN LEADERS AND PEERS

There is no difference between how leaders and peers help others stay accountable.

In low-performing teams, the only person helping team members stay accountable is the manager. In the absence of peer accountability, the manager is sort of expected to do this, so reluctantly they do. High-performing teams have peer accountability. Nobody waits for the boss to do it. If team members feel like another team member needs coaching, it happens and is appreciated. This is what I called "having your back" when I was growing up. High-performing teams have each other's backs!

Patrick Lencioni's book *The Five Dysfunctions of a Team* outlines the root causes of low-performing teams in the workplace. The model uses a pyramid with Dysfunction #1 at the bottom. The dysfunctions are as follows:

- Dysfunction #1: absence of trust
- Dysfunction #2: fear of conflict
- Dysfunction #3: lack of commitment
- Dysfunction #4: avoidance of accountability
- Dysfunction #5: inattention to results

Speaking to the fourth dysfunction—avoidance of accountability—Lencioni notes that when a leader is the only one helping people stay accountable, it's impossible to have a high-functioning team. In fact, you're not a team; you're just a group of people working together, waiting for the boss to point out what needs to be improved. High performance can't exist when the leader has to act as a traffic cop for accountability. A high-performing team has each other's backs and helps each other stay focused on the most important outcomes.

One of the indicators of a high-performing team is when nobody's the boss and you're all perfectly comfortable helping each other stay accountable to shared goals. When team members are just as comfortable pointing out to each other or the leader that they're off track, the leader can fully engage in their role as a member of the team instead of serving as the traffic cop.

Everything I've talked about in this book is meant to cultivate trust, the team's collective IQ, and the exploration of everybody's ideas. These tools allow people to architect their own path to a shared goal, and productively and generously help each other stay accountable.

Most people perceive accountability as the boss's job. High-performing teams view helping others stay accountable as an opportunity, and they feel biting their tongue is tantamount to allowing somebody to walk off the end of the proverbial pier.

Peer accountability is teamwork.

EXERCISE: SHARE PERFORMANCE JOURNALS TO MODEL ACCOUNTABILITY

Teach your team the performance journal process. Then let them know you'll set up a meeting to review one of yours with them.

Journal critically about a recent less-than-satisfying outcome and publish it to your team in advance of the meeting. Ask them to read it and formulate questions.

Meet, debrief, and listen to their perceptions. Ensure they know they don't need to rescue you. The point is to stay accountable.

Ask them for their thoughts, listen actively, and when they are done, say, "Thank you!"

Then invite your team members to begin performance journaling. Ask them to schedule thirty minutes each week to complete a performance journal. Tell them they don't have to share them with anyone, and you don't need proof they are completing them.

Let them know that, from time to time, you will be sharing your journals to drive alignment and so they can help you stay accountable. You can also let them know that if they would ever like to share one of theirs with the team, their vulnerability would be considered heroic!

HELPING OTHERS BE ACCOUNTABLE

It's not cruel; it's a gift. Helping others be accountable isn't reactive; it's proactive. You may have noticed that I don't use the phrase "hold accountable"; instead I keep saying, "Help *stay* accountable." The word "stay" implies that accountability is set up at the beginning of the interaction, not pointed out at the end of a transaction.

Accountability is established in the first discussion through the following steps:

1. The leader outlines where the company needs to go and why.

2. The leader asks the team to come up with the "how" and the "what" by "when."

3. Team members define the "what" by "when."

4. Their commitment is public, active, voluntary, explicit, and mission-based.

5. When making the commitment, they feel completely safe to use the positive power of no.

6. The leader actively listens to their commitment to ensure what they are describing is an accurate depiction of the outcome they are hoping to achieve.

From that first conversation you have positioned each team member to be successfully accountable.

As the leader, you enable your team with the tools to productively facilitate the committed outcome by teaching
them to lead in meetings. You teach them to track commitments in a backlog and provide rich feedback in the
form of coaching to their peers and team members along
the way. You evaluate their progressive outcomes and
inquire curiously when you encounter something that is
unexpected. If necessary, you clarify the desired outcome
and ask for a new plan to get there. Then you repeat the
steps to establish accountability.

PAY ATTENTION TO RESULTS

Lencioni offers another interesting take in *The Five Dysfunctions of a Team* by naming inattention to results as
the fifth dysfunction. At first glance, it doesn't seem like
results could be a fly in the business ointment, but I see
it in most organizations. Everyone is working really hard,
carrying more work than they can feasibly handle, and
most feel that saying no is not an option. When "no" isn't
an option, you can't count on "yes," and people become
adept at coming up with reasons that seem founded for
not hitting targets, deadlines, and so on.

When this happens, it is really easy to get caught up in
the whirlwind of too much work, complex moving parts,
the process, and the excuses. This causes the team to lose
track of the necessary business outcomes and is why it's

critical to have a scoreboard. The scoreboard starts with a 2 × 2 that's prioritized, public, and reviewed regularly so people don't lose sight of the targets. Then commitments need to be tracked in a backlog that is prioritized and reviewed for updates publicly at least once per week.

The backlog becomes your scoreboard and the weekly update becomes a forum to obtain updates, prioritize future work, and address blockers with the team.

EXERCISE: DECLARE AND WORK A BREAKDOWN PUBLICLY WITH YOUR TEAM

The old school of accountability was very focused on a commitment that a person was supposed to keep. The new school is about focusing on the blocker, or the impediment that is in the way of keeping the commitment. This simple shift in focus takes blame off the table and avoids the possibility of anyone conflating the potential breakdown with their character.

The concept of blockers empowers your team members to acknowledge impediments early instead of worrying about letting someone down and failing to live up to their commitments. When you shift the focus to blockers, your team will readily identify them, adjust, and communicate. They will also feel comfortable asking for help early enough for it to make a difference, instead of implementing the old-school approach of exhausting your personal resources before asking for help because you don't want to let anyone down. The old guilt-and-blame paradigm has always burned precious time we don't have in a rapidly changing economy.

Once you introduce the concept of blockers to your team, two things should become true. First, they will begin to feel more comfortable identifying blockers early, coming up with workarounds, adjusting, and communicating their current plans. This is agility at its finest and will lead to fewer missed commitments.

The second thing it gives you is the ability to declare and work a breakdown. Embracing the concept of blockers will minimize the number of missed commitments, but it won't eliminate them. After implementing the concept of blockers and breakdowns, use the first missed commitment or an unexpected result delivered by your team as an opportunity to declare and work a breakdown.

To do this, pull the team together and say something like "I want to have a totally productive, safe meeting. We recently failed to complete some work when and as expected. I would like to work with you to analyze the blockers, unpack the breakdown and learn from it for the purposes of achieving a better outcome in the future." Tell them you are "declaring a breakdown."

Use the meeting rules of engagement that I provided in Chapter 5 at the beginning of the meeting. Then work with your team to explore the situation with curiosity. Reward those team members willing to be vulnerable and own their contributions to the breakdown. Allow them to vent and share their feelings. Then have them come up with ways they can get better results as a team the next time. Get commitments to their future approach.

When you are done working your first breakdown, let them know that they are all free to declare and work breakdowns. Like accountability, if the leader is the only person acknowledging breakdowns, the team isn't working as effectively as it could.

CONCLUSION

THE CADENCE OF
ACCOUNTABILITY

Leadership is about change and change is about people. Changing culture is really about helping people develop new values and new habits in small, incremental baby steps over time. If your team used to value *fast* and now you need them to value *quality*, that requires a whole new set of habits and a new cadence of accountability.

If you want to start using PAVEM to cultivate better commitments from your team, the only way you are going to develop that habit is if you set time aside every day to think about it. Otherwise, you will start out strong and eventually forget about it. When I want to incorporate a new technique into my approach with people, I set up a daily reoccurring meeting with myself for ten minutes to think about it. I think about my upcoming appointments and decide which of them would be a good place to experiment with the technique.

Then I go about my day.

The next day in my ten-minute meeting, I generally realize I forgot to use the new technique and I recommit. Eventually, I start realizing in the moment that I could have used it, then a little more time passes and I *am* using it. When I start using the new technique without even thinking about it and have effectively developed a new habit, I take the meeting off my calendar or replace it with the next habit I want to master.

This same approach works with your team and bigger changes. If you roll out a new process and want the team to start using it, create an agenda item in a weekly reoccurring meeting to evaluate the past week and your team's consistency with the new process. It's likely that you will find there was no consistency with the new process in the first week, but you touched on it. You anchored it to the team, and you will cover it again a week later. Eventually, people will start to remember, they will get consistent, and you will have replaced one cultural habit for a new one. Only new people will need to review the documented process; your existing team will have inculcated it.

Remember, nobody follows process; they follow culture. Even if you have zero documented processes, you have processes. New people will just naturally imitate the habits of your existing team members. Culture is a system of habits. Changing those habits starts with a blueprint or a document. Then the work begins. If you want to change something, create a cadence of accountability and lean hard on the law of diffusion of innovations. When the change you desire has been inculcated, update the agenda with the next change you would like to see.

Keep changing my friends!

To the leader in you!

J. Scott

ACKNOWLEDGMENTS

I want to thank my two children, Jacob and Delaney, for pushing me to be a better leader at home and not just at work. To Todd Friedman, Jake Roig, and Scott Whelan, for my early lessons in leadership. To Dr. Deborah Anderson, for the gift of empathy and my working knowledge of the human brain and our biochemistry.

To Randy Paulson for teaching me that I need people to disagree with me and challenge my ideas. You make me a better leader!

To my team at 120VC, especially Amir Pirastehfar, Andrew Kaiser, Asad Ali, Christeen Hershey, Desi George, Erin Sebastian, Jacki Bricker, Karen Brenneman, Katie Do, Leon Wu, Niloo Karimian, Sandra Wang, Scott Chapman, Steve Diethelm, and Michael Knutson.

To the leadership team I let down, I am truly sorry! Cindy

Schwan, Carlos Garcia, Jim Adams, Kees Steeneken, Ken Walker, Steve Soika, and Lupita Chavaria.

To my CEO coach, Mark Murphy, and Ron Glickman, two leaders I admire.

To my teachers, Simon Sinek, Shawn Achor, Edward Freeman, Raj Sisodia, John Mackey, Brené Brown, Douglas Stone, Fred Kofman, Daniel Pink, William Ury, Daniel Goleman, David Allen, and Ken Blanchard.

To the team at Stagen Leadership Academy and my friends in Picasso and Mandela.

To my Stagen Integral Leadership Program (ILP) Coach, Paul Landraitus.

To Hal and Nikki at Lioncrest Publishing, this book wouldn't be the same without you!

To Erin for the email signatures life hack; that was epic!

And finally, to my clients, for trusting me with their critical projects and their reputations, and for giving me the opportunity to run a company that creates meaningful jobs that my team members love and that leverages its successful business platform to drive positive transformational change in the world. #ConsciousCapitalism

ABOUT THE AUTHOR

J. SCOTT is a father, an entrepreneur, and a philanthropist whose purpose is to inspire people to reach for their potential. He is founder and CEO of the project portfolio leadership and change leadership consultancy 120VC and has been directly responsible for global transformational efforts within organizations such as DirecTV, Trader Joe's, Blizzard Entertainment, Sony Pictures, Mattel, and others. 120VC has enabled his Fortune 100 clients to achieve the value intended from project portfolio management and their enterprise-wide change efforts. His team's approach to change has generated breakthrough results and created meaningful jobs.

33487167R00139

Made in the USA
San Bernardino, CA
23 April 2019